U.S. War Dept. General Staff
141

The Capture of

MAKIN

(*20 November — 24 November 1943*)

American Forces in Action Series

Historical Division
WAR DEPARTMENT   WASHINGTON, D. C.

For sale by the Superintendent of Dcouments, U. S. Government Printing Office
Washington 25, D. C. Price 35 cents

American Forces in Action Series

To Bizerte with the II Corps
(23 April—13 May 1943)

Papuan Campaign: The Buna–Sanananda Operation
(16 November 1942—23 January 1943)

Salerno: American Operations from the Beaches to the Volturno
(9 September—6 October 1943)

Volturno: From the Volturno to the Winter Line
(6 October—15 November 1943)

Merrill's Marauders
(February—May 1944)

Fifth Army at the Winter Line
(15 November 1943—15 January 1944)

Omaha Beachhead
(6 June—13 June 1944)

The Admiralties: Operations of the 1st Cavalry Division
(29 February—18 May 1944)

Guam: Operations of the 77th Division
(21 July—10 August 1944)

The Capture of Makin
(20 November—24 November 1943)

Foreword

In a nation at war, teamwork by the whole people is necessary for victory. But the issue is decided on the battlefield, toward which all national effort leads. The country's fate lies in the hands of its soldier citizens; in the clash of battle is found the final test of plans, training, equipment, and—above all—the fighting spirit of units and individuals.

AMERICAN FORCES IN ACTION SERIES presents detailed accounts of particular combat operations of United States forces. To the American public, this record of high achievement by men who served their nation well is presented as a preface to the full military history of World War II. To the soldiers who took part in the operations concerned, these narratives will give the opportunity to see more clearly the results of orders which they obeyed and of sacrifices which they and their comrades made, in performance of missions that find their meaning in the outcome of a larger plan of battle.

DWIGHT D. EISENHOWER
Chief of Staff

WAR DEPARTMENT
Historical Division
Washington 25, D. C.
18 February 1946

The first full-scale effort to recover from the Japanese some of their strongholds in the Central Pacific was the expedition to the Gilbert Islands in November, 1943. Army, Navy, Marines, and Coast Guard furnished components of the expeditionary forces. The Army elements were commanded by Maj. Gen. Ralph C. Smith. They comprised the 27th Infantry Division Task Force, derived principally from that division but with many provisional units attached. *The Capture of Makin* narrates the Army's part of the campaign, which was the prelude to later advance among the Marshall Islands.

This study is based upon a first narrative prepared in the field from military records and from notes and interviews recorded during the operation by Lt. Col. S. L. A. Marshall. His manuscript has been edited and partially rewritten with the help of additional documentation by Maj. John M. Baker and Dr. George F. Howe. Although in published form the book contains no documentation, the original manuscript, fully documented, is on file in the War Department. One photograph (p. 113) is by the U. S. Coast Guard; the aerials (pp. 10, 38, 51, 52, 58, 78, 82, 102, 114) are by the U. S. Navy. All others were taken by the U. S. Army Signal Corps. Readers are urged to send directly to the Historical Division, War Department, Washington 25, D. C., comments, criticism, and additional information which may be of value in the preparation of a complete and definitive history of the operation at Makin.

DISTRIBUTION:

   AC of S (2); WDSS Div (2); T (Hist Sec) (20); (I&E Off) (1); Base Comd (I&E Off) (1); Def Comd (Hist Sec) (20); FC (I&E Off) (1); Class III Instls (I&E Off) (1); GH ea 25 beds (1); CH ea 25 beds (1); RH ea 25 beds (1); SH ea 25 beds (1); Sp Sv Sch 3–6, 8–11, 17 (10), 2, 7 (20); USMA (80); A (I&E Off) (1); CHQ (I&E Off) (1); D (I&E Off) (1); R (I&E Off) (1); SBn (I&E Off) (1). T/O & E: 8–550, GH ea 25 beds (1); 8–560, SH ea 25 beds (1); Special distribution.

For explanation of distribution formulas see FM 21–6.

AFA–10

Contents

Illustrations

Maps

Charts

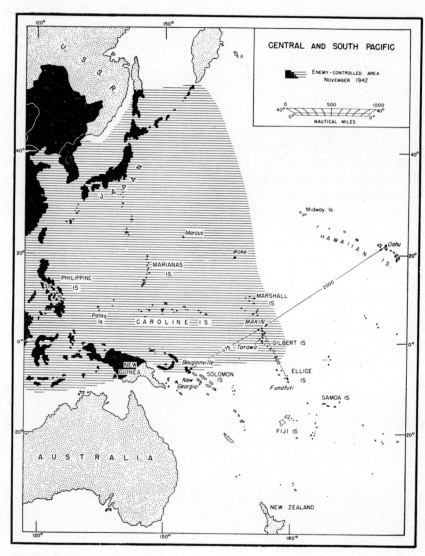

MAP NO. 1

Introduction

BEFORE DAWN ON 20 NOVEMBER 1943, an assemblage of American military might lay waiting off the western shore of Makin, northernmost atoll in the Gilbert Islands (Map No. 2, page 2). A strong task force, with transports carrying men of the U. S. Army, was about to commence the assault on Makin. Off Tarawa, about 105 miles to the south, an even larger force of U. S. Marines was poised in readiness to seize the airfield and destroy the Japanese there. From points as distant as the Hawaiian Islands and New Zealand, and by several different routes, the separate elements of this armada had gathered to carry out our first aggressive mission in the Central Pacific. The attack upon Makin would be the first seizure of an atoll by an Army landing force.

Invasion of the Gilbert Islands brought the war in the Central Pacific to a new phase. After almost two years of defense, of critical engagements like the Battle of Midway (3–6 June 1942) and hit-and-run raids like those against Makin (17 August 1942) and Wake Island (24 December 1942), the United Nations were taking the offensive. They were to do in that area what had been done for a year in the Southwest Pacific. The attack upon the Gilberts was for the Central Pacific the counterpart of that upon the Solomons (7 August 1942) in the Southwest Pacific. Japanese-held bases were to be recovered and used against the enemy in further strikes toward the heart of his empire. (Map No. 1, page viii.)

For almost a year after the Battle of Midway, the strength of the United Nations had permitted aggressive action in only one Pacific area at a time. Then, in the Aleutians, Attu had been seized in May 1943, and Kiska had been occupied in August, while the Japanese were also being driven from their bases in the Solomons and New Georgia. With the threat to the western coast of Canada

1

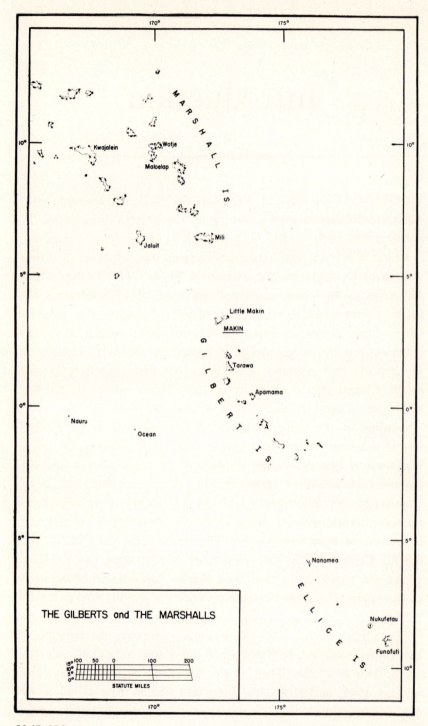

THE GILBERTS and THE MARSHALLS

STATUTE MILES

MAP NO. 2

and the United States removed, force became available for simultaneous campaigns in Bougainville and the Gilberts. On 1 November, the hard battle for Bougainville was opened; at the same time, the expedition to the Gilberts was starting on its mission. We were ready to clear what Admiral Chester W. Nimitz called "another road to Tokyo."

The Gilberts straddle the equator some 2,000 miles southwest of Oahu (Map No. 2, page 2). Most of them are low, coral atolls, rising a few feet from the sea, supporting coconut palms, breadfruit trees, mangroves, and sand brush. Two genuine islands, Ocean and Nauru, were included in the days of British control in the same colonial administrative unit with the atolls, although they lay some 200 to 400 miles farther west. The Japanese seized Makin on 10 December 1941 and converted it into a seaplane base. In September 1942 they occupied Tarawa and Apamama. At Tarawa they built an air strip and collected a considerable garrison. There also they set up administrative headquarters for the naval forces in the Gilberts. On Apamama an observation outpost was established. On Ocean and Nauru Islands they also built up air bases, and from the latter extracted phosphates important in their munitions industry. Combined with these Japanese bases were others in the Marshalls to the northwest, the whole comprising an interlocking system of defense.

If the Gilberts and Marshalls were outer defenses of the conquered island empire of Japan, for Americans they were a menace to the fundamental line of communications from Hawaii to Australia. From them, the Japanese struck at our advanced staging positions, such as Canton Island and Funafuti in the Ellice Islands. From them also, Japanese observation planes could report the movements of our convoys and task forces, could direct submarines and bombers to points of interception, and thus hold in the Central Pacific area a large portion of our fighting strength to furnish adequate protection. Once the islands had come into our hands, our route to the Southwest Pacific could be shortened sufficiently to provide, in effect, the equivalent of added shipping for the transport of men and matériel.

Raids by bombers of a U. S. Navy task force brought Makin under fire in January 1942. In the following August Carlson's Marine Raiders spent an active night there destroying installations and most of the small Japanese garrison. In the first nine months of 1943, Seventh Air Force planes harassed the Japanese in the Marshalls and Gilberts and measured their growing strength. While American forces were pursuing this program of harassment, their power to strike aggressively was also growing.

It was apparent to the Joint Chiefs of Staff by July 1943 that our war potential had reached a level permitting more than neutralizing raids against the islands; we could attempt to take them. On 20 July they sent orders to the Commander-in-Chief, Pacific Ocean Areas, covering operations in the Ellice and Gilbert Islands groups, including Nauru. They estimated that enough amphibious and ground forces would be available, without hampering the operations already under way in the South and Southwest Pacific, or delaying those projected for early in 1944 against Wewak, Manus, and Kavieng. Two Marine divisions and one Army division, with supplementary defense and construction troops, and a considerable surface force, were deemed necessary. The target date was set tentatively for 15 November, contingent upon ability to gather naval forces from the North and South Pacific and assault shipping from the North Pacific in time.[1] Strategically this attack would aid operations elsewhere by putting the enemy under pressure in a new area, and it would secure our lines of communication to the Solomons; as the Joint Chiefs of Staff set forth its purposes, it would also be of help in gaining control of the Marshalls in the following January.

The command was to be as specified by Admiral Nimitz, Commander-in-Chief, Pacific Ocean Areas. Planning and organization for a series of operations in the Central Pacific Area began at once. A force uniting land, sea, and air power in flexible proportions, adapted to the successive requirements of a series of island conquests, was constituted.[2] From base to beaches, the Navy would transport and protect the troops, and it would support their subsequent operations by naval gunfire and carrier-based planes. Troops for the assault and others for the garrisons which would convert captured islands to American bases were to be drawn from both the Marines and the Army. The troops were to be organized as the V Amphibious Corps.

---

[1] This was just before the action at Kiska.

[2] The V Amphibious Force, under naval command, was that which operated in the Central Pacific Area.

Preparations were initiated for an attack upon the Gilberts, an operation in which the organization would receive its first test in combat. When this operation had succeeded, other campaigns would extend the road to Tokyo further to the northwest. The route would run via Kwajalein, Eniwetok, Saipan, and Guam, to Iwo Jima, Okinawa, and beyond. The Gilberts were only the first barrier to surmount; the goal was Tokyo itself.

MAJ. GEN. RALPH C. SMITH, *Commanding General, 27th Infantry Division, United States Army, and of the landing forces at Makin.*

Preparing the Attack

The Planning Begins

THE ATTACK UPON THE GILBERT ISLANDS was an early experience in amphibious operations and the first atoll operation in the Central Pacific Area. Men, matériel, and methods were chosen in a series of crucial decisions by a planning staff which had to anticipate every aspect of the operation. Once the landing forces arrived at their objectives, 2,000 miles from base, they had to win with what they brought.

Planning was undertaken by several staff groups. The general staff of the Commanding General, Central Pacific Area, that of the Commander-in-Chief, Pacific Ocean Areas (CinCPOA), and that of the 27th Infantry Division were all implicated. The staff of the 27th Division were acquainted with their mission in a joint conference with the staff of CinCPOA, early in August 1943, and set about studying a reorganization to fit its requirements. The whole operation was given the code name *Galvanic,* and the Army portion was designated as *Kourbash.* Tarawa, Nauru, and Apamama were first selected as the objectives. The Army's mission was to be Nauru. For the next two months, 27th Division planning centered upon Nauru.

Analysis of the naval problems eventually caused the original mission to be shifted from Nauru to Makin. Nauru lay so far to the west that a supporting naval force there would be dangerously separated from another committed at Tarawa and Apamama. A great tactical advantage would thus be offered to any strong, intercepting Japanese force. Nauru was also so large and well defended that a larger body of troops than could be transported would be needed to gain possession of it. The decision to confine the operation to the central Gilberts was made known to 27th Division Headquarters

7

on 28 September. Abruptly its planning was transferred to capturing Makin. Only six weeks remained in which to get ready.

The new mission required redefinition of the force necessary. On 29 August a first draft of a reorganized 27th Division Landing Force had been submitted to the Commanding General, Central Pacific Area, calling for attachment to the division of several units to assist in landing operations and to support the ensuing action. This draft had to be amended. Previous planning was not entirely wasted but its revision had to be complete. The submarine *Nautilus,* with the 27th Division's assistant G–2, Capt. Donald M. Neuman, aboard, cruised in the vicinity of Makin, taking through the periscope rolls of pictures which included the entire west shore of Makin. Mosaics from the Seventh Air Force photographic reconnaissance flights of 23 July 1942, 20 February 1943, and 11 July 1943, and pictures taken during a raid by carrier-based planes on 18–19 September 1943, were used to establish the strength and position of enemy defenses. The report of the Marines (Carlson's Raiders) on their night invasion

MAP NO. 3

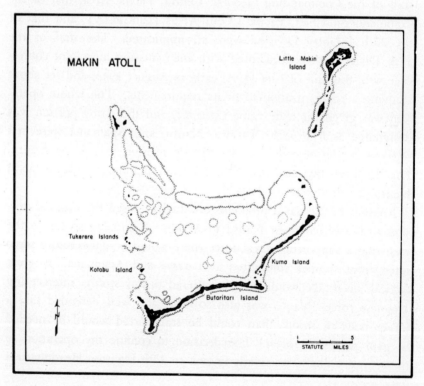

of 16/17 August 1942 added more useful data. To Oahu came two former residents at Makin, Lt. Comdr. Heyen of the Royal Australian Navy and Pvt. Fred C. Narruhn of the 1st Fiji Infantry. The latter had been born on Makin; both were to accompany the expedition. With these new sources of information, new plans were devised which fitted the conditions at Makin.

Makin Atoll

Makin atoll is an irregular formation of reefs and islands around a large lagoon, approximately triangular in shape (Map No. 3, page 8). The northern side is a reef 17 miles long, running east and west between islands. The western side, about 14 miles from tip to tip, consists of small islands, a reef broken by several channels into the lagoon, and the western end of Butaritari Island. The remainder of Butaritari, and the island of Kuma northeast of it, stretch for some 13 miles to the eastern corner of the atoll.

The main passage into the lagoon runs through the reef at its southwest corner, passing just north of the northwestern tip of Butaritari. Another near the northern corner is sufficiently deep but is almost blocked by islets in the lagoon. Other channels are suitable only for small boats. Numerous islets are scattered about the inland water, so that navigational difficulties and beach conditions alike favor the use of the southwestern portion for anchorage.

None of the other islands is as large or important as Butaritari, on which the Japanese had developed a seaplane base. Butaritari is shaped like a long, bending ribbon; its western end resembles a fishtail, or the armrest of a crutch, with two main points projecting westward from the central shore, forming there a shallow curve. As one goes eastward from this shore, the main body of the island narrows abruptly. It averages 500 yards from ocean to lagoon, and at some points is much less. Butaritari and Kuma are connected by a reef, one side of which is high enough to permit crossing on foot at low tide.

Heavy surf beats on the southern shore of Butaritari, exposed as it is to the open sea. (See illustration, p. 10.) From the northern shore, where the water is quieter, a wide reef covered with sticky mud extends into the lagoon from 500 to 1,500 feet. At the western end of the island the smoother sections of the beach are very widely

separated from each other, and narrow, while jagged coral pinnacles make an approach to them an occasion for dexterous navigation. They are freer of heavy surf than the southern beaches and were believed during the planning for the attack on Makin to offer suitable access, regardless of the coral obstacles, to the island itself. The Navy, whose task it would be to convey the assault troops to the

10

BUTARITARI *from the southwest as seen from navy bombers open-*
ing the action on D Day. At left are Red Beach 1 (A) and Red Beach
2 (B). The West Tank Barrier clearing (W) and Yellow Beach
(Y) appear at right. Later site of our artillery on Ukiangong Point (U).

beaches, was satisfied that "landing boats could get ashore there
at any time." The lagoon reef was also deemed to be no obstacle.
"LST's (Landing Ship, Tank) could stem the edge of **the** reef at
low water springs, to effect the direct landing of vehicles. LCI's
(Landing Craft, Infantry), dukws, and Alligators could get ashore
at all states of tides," according to their estimate.

The islands are so flat that they afford no natural points of observation, and so low that after rains, extensive areas, especially in the west, are covered by shallow ponds surrounded by marshland (Map No. 4, p. 13). Butaritari and Kuma Islands were those on which the natives lived the year around. Before the war copra had been the principal export; coconut palms are widely dispersed but at various points so predominant as to seem like cultivated groves. For food the natives raise *bobai* plants, which they grow in pits.

Bobai pits were known to be more numerous near the villages. With soft banks and mucky bottoms from which the vegetation rose several feet to a level approximating that of the growth around them, these pits were recognized as substantial obstacles to foot soldiers and tanks. Their exact locations were unknown. Elsewhere, especially along the lagoon shore and at the edges of the ponds, mangroves and salt brush are found. The terrain seemed likely to limit vehicles more than it would the foot soldiers, who could move forward under the ceiling of coconut palm branches or through the clearings and marshes, even if with difficulty. Inland from the western shore the firmest route for vehicles was the island highway and the lagoon beach. At low tide the reef itself is bared and could be used for the passage of wheeled vehicles.

The island's main highway is unpaved and narrow at most points. Crossing the marshes it resembles a causeway bordered by coconut palms. In the villages which it connects, it widens to two lanes along the grass-roofed huts. It is made of coral sand and is well-drained. From Ukiangong village on the southwestern point, it runs northeastward to the lagoon shore and along that to the eastern end of the island; its route passes, therefore, through Butaritari village, near the island anchorage, across the bases of the four wharves which jut into the lagoon near the anchorage, and through the eastern village of Tanimaiaki. About 1,700 islanders, Melanesian and Polynesian, were known to live on Butaritari and Kuma, and with them, before the arrival of the Japanese, a score of Europeans and half-castes. Scattered hamlets are connected with the main highway by secondary roads and trails. In the central portion of the island, such a narrow, unsurfaced road runs close along the ocean shore, and is connected with the main highway by cross-island roads. Paths and trails branch out to points and coves, but except for a few, their location was not known to the invaders before the occupation.

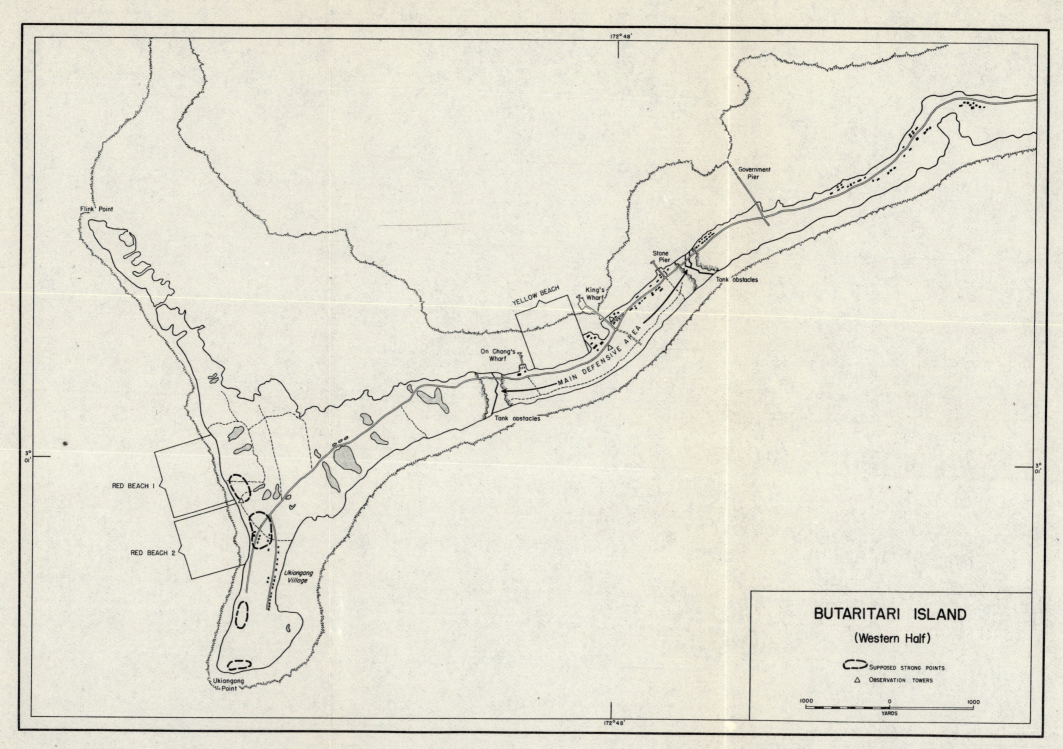

Flink Point

YELLOW BEACH

King's
Wharf

On Chong's
Wharf

MAIN DEFENSIVE AREA

Tank obstacles

Stone
Pier

Tank obstacles

Government
Pier

RED BEACH I

RED BEACH 2

Ukiangong
Village

Ukiangong
Point

172° 48'

172° 48'

3°
01'

3°
01'

BUTARITARI ISLAND

(Western Half)

⬭ SUPPOSED STRONG POINTS

△ OBSERVATION TOWERS

1000   0   1000
YARDS

Air photographs of Butaritari Island revealed certain features very clearly. About 3,000 yards from the western end of the island lay a clearing from lagoon to ocean, a bare strip within which an anti-tank trap had been dug for most of its length. Its counterpart lay eastward approximately two more miles, crossing the island somewhat west of its center. Between these two clearings the Japanese were known to have concentrated their principal installations and to have built their main defenses. Between them, also pushing out into the lagoon, the photographs showed three wharves of varying length, while a fourth, east of the easternmost clearing, ran from a point outside the fortified area.

The westernmost pier runs from a base about 300 yards east of the West Tank Barrier. Known as On Chong's Wharf, it was built like the others by the British as a high-water structure, for it extends only 400 feet and is unusable at low tide. One thousand yards further east is King's Wharf, the main structure, projecting 1,000 feet into the lagoon and thus clearing the reef. At its tip it has several spurs, to one of which the Japanese attached two seaplane ramps. Between its base and that of On Chong's Wharf, a wide sandspit protrudes sufficiently to create a small cove rimmed by a smooth sandy beach adjacent to King's Wharf. Some 800 yards farther east, the third wharf springs from a wide base. Like On Chong's Wharf, this structure, which was known as Stone Pier, is dry at low tides, for it is only 500 feet long. At the base of each of the wharves and on the sandspit were buildings, some of which had been erected in the days of British occupation. A concrete church which had protected Carlson's Raiders from Japanese light gunfire lies about 200 yards southwest of Stone Pier, and a long concrete native hospital is located along the beach northeast of Stone Pier.

A fourth pier, long, but of inferior construction and damaged by storms, was left outside the "citadel" area by the Japanese when they planned the fortifications. Although it stretched 1,750 feet into the lagoon from a point 1,250 yards eastward from Stone Pier, it had not seemed worth repairing and using. The East Tank Barrier was therefore constructed just beyond the base of Stone Pier, about 1,000 yards short of this Government Wharf.

In the buildings around the base of Stone Pier, Carlson's Raiders found a center of Japanese activity on the night of their raid (16/17 August, 1942). In the period since that destructive visitation, the

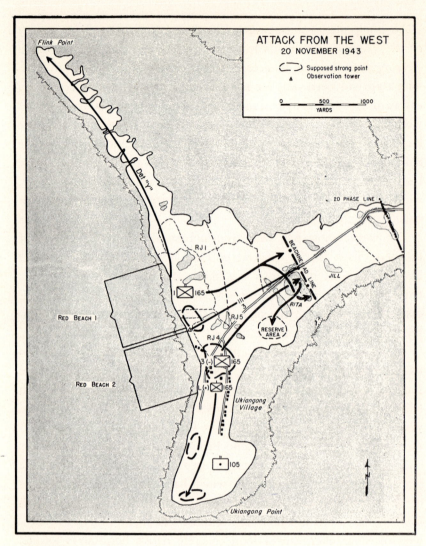

ATTACK FROM THE WEST
20 NOVEMBER 1943

Supposed strong point
Observation tower

0   500   1000
YARDS

MAP NO. 5

Japanese had greatly increased their installations and defenses, but the trees and other concealment left the exact character of these works to be ascertained by the invaders in the course of the assault.

The aerial photographs also showed two sharp indentations of the ocean shore. On the eastern side of Ukiangong Point, the southwestern projection of Butaritari, a wide, deep bay has been worn. Again, at almost the exact midway point in the southern coast, the ocean has carved out a deep Bight, averaging over 100 yards in width and extending inward 600 yards. At this point, therefore, the width

14

of the island is reduced to 150 yards, despite the projection of a knob into the lagoon opposite one part of the Bight.

Although estimates of the number of Japanese forces on Makin varied, the 27th Division anticipated finding there 800 troops, operating 4 heavy and 4 medium antiaircraft guns, from 20 to 40 machine guns, and the rifles of one company. The enemy's prepared positions were understood to be in the area south of the wharves between the two tank barrier defense systems, and in an outer perimeter paralleling the shore at the western end of Butaritari. The operations' overlay map for invasion from the Red Beaches circled four strongpoints at fairly regular intervals from the land separating the two Red Beaches to the southwestern point (Map No. 5, p. 14). Ukiangong village was also reported to be the site of military activity, probably defended by several machine guns.

The proximity of Makin to the airfields and seaplane bases at Tarawa, Mili, Jaluit, Maloelap, Wotje, Nauru, and Kwajalein made enemy air strikes from them a possibility. At Makin itself observers on the submarine *Nautilus* had found considerable air activity in October. Invasion there would thus be carried to success only if enemy airpower had been neutralized by blows at his bases or by interception and antiaircraft during the operation.

Weather conditions suitable for air operations could be expected for at least part of November. Normally, weather changes in the equatorial belt are slow and are predictable for several weeks in advance. When the equatorial front moves south it introduces a period of doldrum weather. The limitless ceiling and excellent visibility which prevail before this change would not only aid bombing operations but would deny cover to the Japanese either for air raids or for an approach by units of their fleet. Naval operations would also derive benefit from the conditions which could be expected for much of November, since the steady easterly winds furnished an isothermal belt of surface water conducive to good sound-detection of enemy submarines. After the doldrum period the prevailing winds upon Makin would become strong westerlies, making landing on the western beaches impossible.

Four miles east of Makin lay Little Makin, a satellite atoll of small proportions on which Japanese outpost installations might exist, but on which no significant military activity had been noted in reconnaissance by air and submarine (Map No. 3, p. 8).

To fulfill the mission of capturing Makin and eliminating the Japanese required: first, an attack upon the island which contained their prepared positions; secondly, control of Kuma and other smaller islands on which outposts might be placed; and finally, pursuit of the enemy to all the lesser points of refuge for enemy troops which might flee from Butaritari. As a precautionary measure, it also involved early air reconnaissance over Little Makin and the possible dispatch of a small force. Possession of the captured atoll might then be transferred to a garrison force whose mission it would be to convert Makin from a Japanese seaplane base to an American station for shore-based airplanes. The major field of operations for the invaders was necessarily the island of Butaritari.

The Tactical Plan

Landings at Makin and Tarawa, 105 miles away, were planned to begin simultaneously by two separate landing forces from Task Force 54, Rear Adm. Richmond K. Turner, commanding. Arrayed with them as elements of the Task Force were support and air support groups, a minesweeper group, transport and LST groups, and a garrison force. At 0830, 20 November 1943, the first landing craft were to touch the beach at each atoll. While the 27th Division Landing Team, with attached units, took Makin, the 2d Marine Division was to assault Tarawa, leaving one of its combat teams in reserve for the support of one or both operations. If this reserve remained uncommitted, it was later to occupy Apamama.

The assaulting force at Makin was to consist of the 165th RCT, less the 2d BLT, which was designated as a reserve landing force during the first stage. Once the beachheads were secure, command would pass from Admiral Turner to the senior troop commander and would apply to all shore-based land, sea, and air forces. When capture was complete, command of the island was to be transmitted to the garrison force commander, and the landing force was to be removed.

The plans adopted by the Northern Landing Force employed overwhelming strength in every arm against an enemy whose known positions were to be bombarded and then enveloped. Instead of delivering an assault of maximum power at any one point, the schedule called for two separate landings, one following the other after an

16

interval of about two hours. The western beaches were designated as Red Beach 1 and Red Beach 2, and on them, at 0830, the 1st and 3d BLT's were to commence penetrating the island side by side, each being led by a special landing group in 16 Alligators. If all went well according to plan on the Red Beaches, at 1030 a second landing was to be made on the lagoon shore, among the piers, on what was known as Yellow Beach (Map No. 4, p. 13).

The second landing was to be made by the 2d BLT, following to the beach another special landing group, and was to be supported by the medium tanks of Company A, 193d Tank Battalion and their 75-mm guns. If the first landing met with unexpectedly successful opposition, the landing on Yellow Beach could be postponed and instead, the 2d BLT would be committed in support of the other two battalions on the Red Beaches.

Bombers of the Seventh Air Force, temporarily operating under Navy control, were to soften up the island during the week preceding the attack, to provide photographic reconnaissance on the last day before the attack, and to strike Nauru and air strips in the Marshalls from which the Japanese might send aid during the action to their force on Butaritari. Navy carrier-based bombers would support the landing operations, dropping half-ton and one-ton demolition bombs and one-ton "daisy-cutters" for the first half-hour of daylight upon coast artillery positions, heavy antiaircraft guns, pillboxes, housing installations, stores, and personnel. They were to strike first the area from the West Tank Barrier eastward to the vicinity of Government Wharf. At 0615 this activity was to cease, but the carrier planes would maintain daylight air patrols, submarine reconnaissance, morning and afternoon search flights, artillery spotting, observation liaison, and light bombing and strafing as needed throughout the operation.

At 0620, prearranged naval bombardment would begin according to a firing plan devised by collaboration of Army and Navy staffs. Striking first with the 14-inch guns of the four battleships and the 8-inch guns of three cruisers, this devastating attack was to rake the western shore from Kotabu Island to Ukiangong Point and to fall upon key points back from the beach. If need be, the range might be narrowed to 2,000 yards. A second bombardment was to be directed from 0850 to 1025 upon the area between the tank barriers and from lagoon to ocean shore. During this preparation for a second landing, a zone of safety was established between beachhead line and

17

West Tank Barrier into which only patrols might advance before the barrage was lifted. The prearranged firing plan called for a total of 1,990 rounds of 14-inch, 1,645 rounds of 8-inch, and 7,490 rounds of 5-inch shells from four battleships, four cruisers, and six destroyers: in all, 1,717 tons of projectiles. Half the shells were fitted with delayed-action fuzes to permit penetration among the thick coconuts before detonation.

When the first wave of boats was 800 yards from the Red Beaches (according to schedule, at 0825), carrier-based fighters were to strafe the beaches and the area 100 yards inland and 500 yards north and south of the beaches' extremities. Then, as the boats reached a point 100 yards from the shore, the fighters were to withdraw while bombers returned to hit every defense installation within 500 yards to 1,000 yards inland from the beaches, all the way across the island from north to south. They were also to strike every evident activity on Ukiangong Point, paying particular attention to mortars, pillboxes, and installations which could register on the Red Beaches, and using 100-lb. and 500-lb. demolition and fragmentation bombs.

Fifteen minutes after the first wave had landed (if the schedule were strictly adhered to, at 0845), the bombers were to yield the field to the naval gunners. At 0850, the warships would resume scheduled fire upon tank barriers, gun positions, and the highway.

The same pattern of bombardment, strafing, and bombing was to precede the attack at Yellow Beach, but there, extra caution was needed to avoid dropping bombs among friendly troops.

Both the BLT's landing on the western beaches at 0830 were to advance as rapidly as possible to a division beachhead line which crossed the island about 1,600 yards ahead in an area of swamps and pools. The accompanying light tanks were expected to devote particular attention to destroying the enemy strongpoints believed to lie just inland from the beaches. When the two BLT's had reached the line, the unit on the left, it was thought, would have crossed easier terrain against less resistance. It was therefore quickly to reor-

ALLIGATORS AT MAKIN *were used to carry the first assault troops ashore, to convey wounded to the transports, serve as ferries from barges unable to clear the reefs, and take troops on special trips to outlying islands. Here one drags a pallet to Yellow Beach at low tide.*

ganize, extend across the island, and take over the whole line while the 3d BLT at the right would drop back and go into divisional reserve. Patrols were to be sent forward after reaching the line but the second phase of advance was to wait until 1030. Thus the advancing 1st BLT would keep clear of naval shells falling near the West Tank Barrier during the prearranged fire before the Yellow Beach landings.

Within the zone of each BLT invading from the west lay one of the island's projections, Flink Point at the left and Ukiangong Point at the right (Map No. 4, p. 13). The special detachments from the 3d Battalion, 105th Infantry, which were borne ashore in LVT's

(Landing Vehicle, Tracked), popularly called "Alligators," were to move at once to the flanks and there establish positions defending the beaches. Only one platoon was to man the position on the left flank of Red Beach, the remainder proceeding out the narrow Flink Point, over a shallow water passage which separated part of it from the remainder, and clearing all hostile forces. At the southern end of the western beaches, on the right flank of Red Beach 2, the special detachment was to leave one platoon in charge of the position while the remainder joined Company L, 165th Infantry, and light tanks of the 193d Tank Battalion in clearing Ukiangong Point to its tip.

Batteries of antiaircraft artillery (93d Coast Artillery (AA) less automatic weapons platoons) formed part of each of the BLT's, going in over the Red Beaches. Additional antiaircraft protection was to arrive on D + 1 when a provisional antiaircraft battalion of the 98th Coast Artillery (AA) came to serve as part of both the assault and garrison forces. It was to remain in floating reserve, prepared to land on divisional order.

The field artillery batteries which went ashore with the BLT's were to pass at once from battalion control and to take positions obtained for them on Ukiangong Point. From there they were to deliver supporting call fire upon any point under attack during the first day or two.

While the larger assault from the west was in its first stage, a special landing detachment in two landing craft was to take Kotabu Island, off Flink Point (Map No. 3, p. 8). A platoon of marines with a reinforced infantry platoon from Company G, 165th Infantry, was to execute this mission after preparatory naval bombardment of the little island. The detail was to destroy the enemy forces found there, and on any of the other islets on the western side of the Makin triangular lagoon. Passage between the island and Flink Point would thus be secured from close-range enemy fire. If the landings at Red Beach succeeded, that scheduled for Yellow Beach could then take place.

At W Hour (fixed on D Day at 1030) the 2d BLT was to arrive at Yellow Beach, following a special landing group in Alligators. The landing group was to divide into two detachments each of which would go to one of the flanks, clear the enemy from the base of the wharf there, and set up a beach block and defensive position. The 2d BLT, once it was ashore, was to reorganize and move southward, cutting across the island from lagoon to ocean. While part of the assault would then become a holding action on the left, the main effort would be on the right toward the West Tank Barrier. Since the 1st BLT would be advancing eastward, the barrier would be enveloped from front and rear. When that fortification had been taken the holding action on the left would be superseded by a strong drive eastward the length of the island, traversing the narrow, twisting ribbon of marsh and grove to its last sharp point. Special landing parties would be detached for the seizure of any outpost islands and the destruction of enemy units.

A feature of the plan was the availability, by afternoon, of supporting howitzer fire from the field artillery battalion on Ukiangong Point. (See illustration, p. 10.) It was to cover any part of the main defensive area on call and was expected to be of great value, especially if the preparatory bombardment had not fully neutralized Japanese defenses. Such was the structure of the tactical plan for the operation on Makin.

Training and Equipping the Attacking Force

The Northern Landing Force was comprised of 6,470 officers and enlisted men. They were accompanied by 150 garrison force troops, 10 correspondents, and 6 observers. The total size was controlled by available transport facilities and the mission's nature. The latter was uppermost in determining the composition of the force. Since the initial tactical units were BLT's, the battalion headquarters elements were larger than normal. Other noteworthy increases were among engineer and signal personnel. Elsewhere, including division headquarters, drastic reductions were the rule. Rifle companies were cut, although not uniformly, to about 150 men. Addition of a ship's party of one company from the 105th Infantry to each battalion of the 165th Infantry made each BLT seem larger than normal in spite of the reduction of rifle company strength. The three BLT's were not uniform either, the range extending from 42 to 58 officers and from 917 to 1,161 men. Battalion medical detachments and the divisional collecting unit were cut down enough to permit the sending to Makin of a surgical team, 3 officers and 33 men, without enlarging the total medical personnel. This gave the landing force equipment

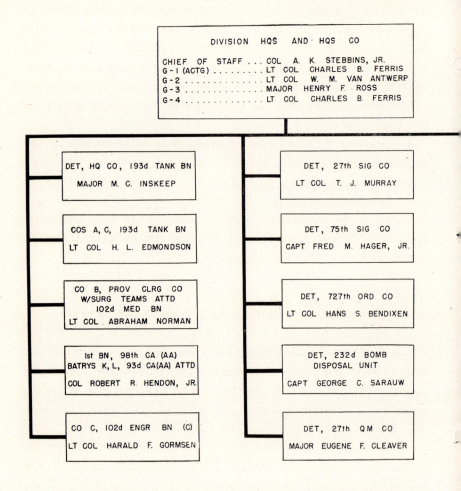

DIVISION HQS AND HQS CO

CHIEF OF STAFF ... COL A. K. STEBBINS, JR.
G - 1 (ACTG) .... LT COL CHARLES B. FERRIS
G - 2 .... LT COL W. M. VAN ANTWERP
G - 3 .... MAJOR HENRY F. ROSS
G - 4 .... LT COL CHARLES B. FERRIS

DET, HQ CO, 193d TANK BN
MAJOR M. C. INSKEEP

DET, 27th SIG CO
LT COL T. J. MURRAY

COS A, C, 193d TANK BN
LT COL H. L. EDMONDSON

DET, 75th SIG CO
CAPT FRED M. HAGER, JR.

CO B, PROV CLRG CO
W/SURG TEAMS ATTD
102d MED BN
LT COL ABRAHAM NORMAN

DET, 727th ORD CO
LT COL HANS S. BENDIXEN

1st BN, 98th CA (AA)
BATRYS K, L, 93d CA(AA) ATTD
COL ROBERT R. HENDON, JR.

DET, 232d BOMB
DISPOSAL UNIT
CAPT GEORGE C. SARAUW

CO C, 102d ENGR BN (C)
LT COL HARALD F. GORMSEN

DET, 27th QM CO
MAJOR EUGENE F. CLEAVER

¹ COMMAND OF THE REGIMENT PASSED TO LT COL KELLEY WHEN COL CONROY DIED IN ACTION, 20 NOV. 1943.

CHART NO. 1

FORCE (52.6) AT MAKIN
RALPH C. SMITH

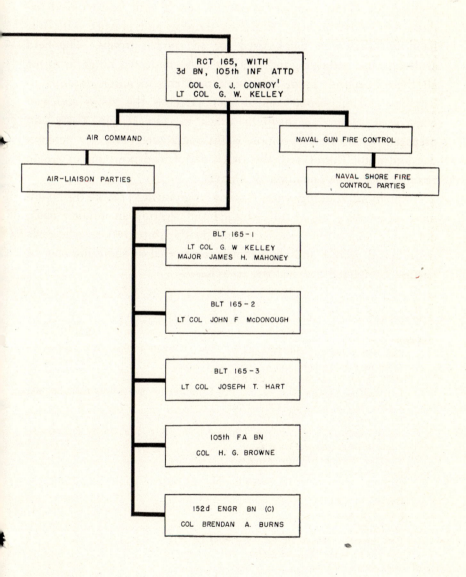

RCT 165, WITH
3d BN, 105th INF ATTD
COL G. J. CONROY[1]
LT COL G. W. KELLEY

AIR COMMAND

NAVAL GUN FIRE CONTROL

AIR-LIAISON PARTIES

NAVAL SHORE FIRE
CONTROL PARTIES

BLT 165-1
LT COL G. W KELLEY
MAJOR JAMES H. MAHONEY

BLT 165-2
LT COL JOHN F McDONOUGH

BLT 165-3
LT COL JOSEPH T. HART

105th FA BN
COL H. G. BROWNE

152d ENGR BN (C)
COL BRENDAN A. BURNS

for an advanced hospital with full surgical service, an innovation in Pacific warfare at this stage. Of the 6,470 men in the force, approximately 1,300 were in units which had been attached to the 27th Division for this operation.[1]

Although the 27th Division had anticipated taking part in some aggressive operation in the Central Pacific Area, and had trained for beach landings and jungle fighting since coming to the Hawaiian Islands, the imminent arrival of actual combat encouraged intensive training for Makin. Jungle woodcraft, jungle lore, and tropical hygiene were now studied. Weapons training and practice with live hand grenades were emphasized for all combat troops. The field artillery, tank battalion, and infantry each conducted range firing of all their weapons. From small unit problems in jungle fighting to battalion and regimental combat team exercises, the troops reviewed what was involved in daylight attack in close terrain, hasty and prepared defenses of a position, night operations, perimeter defense, day and night withdrawal, the attack of fortified positions in jungle terrain, and the elimination of snipers.

Amphibious training with floating equipment, practice in swimming and staying afloat fully clothed and wearing an infantry pack, unloading and loading supplies, and finally, ship-to-shore rehearsals under naval gunfire and air bombing, controlled by shore fire control parties, completed the realistic exercises.

---

[1] Components were as follows:
    Det., Hq & Hq Co, 27th Division
    165th RCT (Co's I, K, and L, 105th Inf attached)
    193d Tk Bn (Less Dets. and Co B)
    LST Landing Groups Nos. 31, 78, 179 (consisting of Det., 193d Tank Bn, and Dets. X, Y, Z, 3d Bn, 105th Inf)
    152d Engr Bn (C)
    1st Bn, 98th CA (AA), 90-mm (Btrys A(S/L), B, C, and D) Atchd: Btrys K and L, 93d CA (AA) (AW)
    4th Plat, V Amphib Corps Rcn Co
    Det., 27th Sig Co
    Det., 75th Sig Co
    Det., 727th Ord Co
    Det., 27th QM Co
    Det., AAF
    Co C and Det., Hq & Hq Co, 102d Engr Bn (C)
    Det., 232d Bomb Disposal Unit
    Signal Photo Section
    Naval Shore Fire Control Parties

General Ralph C. Smith and some of his staff were convinced that the initial forces to cross the beaches of Makin should be carried ashore in LVT's (Alligators), amphibian tractors capable of self-propulsion on water and on land. Each of the 3 landing groups which first approached the 3 separate beaches on Butaritari was to ride in 16 Alligators. To operate the vehicles, personnel was drawn from the Headquarters Company of a tank battalion.

Behind this first element in the invading forces they planned to send a platoon of light tanks, and, on Yellow Beach, an additional force of medium tanks. These heavy units would be brought to shallow water by LCT's (Landing Craft, Tanks), blunt-nosed lighters of relatively shallow draft.

A detail of the 193d Tank Battalion began working with the landing teams on 15 October to develop the skill needed to operate and maintain Alligators. They had but one LVT on which to practice, and when those for the Makin landings were delivered on 30 October, they were of a longer, later type, lacking not only armor but necessary armament. They had to be conditioned for use in great haste while machine-gun mounts were obtained for them by stripping some of the armed vehicles on Oahu. Time for training with the transports was very short indeed.

Time was also insufficient for infantry and tank crews to achieve adequate effectiveness in cooperation before the actual operation began. Communication between crews inside the tanks and infantry-men outside them was an unsolved problem; another was the method by which infantry officers could bring tanks directly into support.

Matériel and supplies for the Northern Landing Force were, like the force itself, controlled by available transport and by the nature of the mission. The expedition was equipped with jeeps and trucks, but in numbers deeply cut from the Tables of Basic Allowances in order to save both their room and that of fuel to operate them.

The communications plans required, in addition to telephone and telegraph sets, switchboards, miles of wire on reels of various types, and a considerable quantity of radio equipment. Radio sets were to link the various levels of command, afloat and ashore, the infan-try, field artillery, naval gunfire, air, and tank support, the beach parties, and the air observers. They ranged in size from the 6-lb. portable SCR–536 to the 275-lb. SCR–608, and the trailer-borne SCR–299. Two radar sets were brought to furnish air warning.

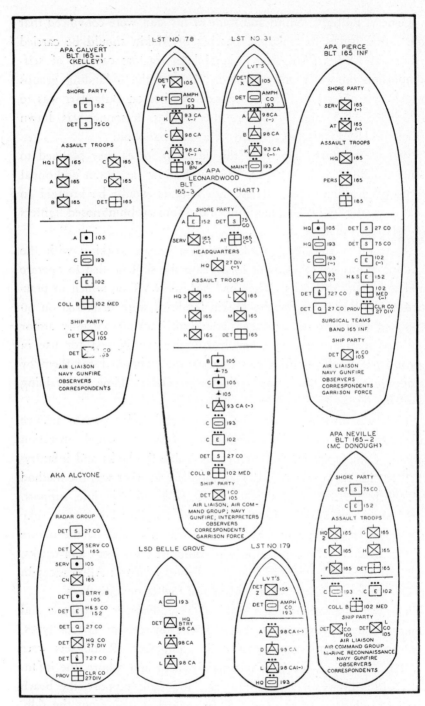

CHART NO. 2 Loading Plan

To clear beaches, haul supplies, and draw artillery pieces into position, 38 tractor bulldozers were taken by the attacking force. Of these, two D–7's and four R–4's were for use at each of the three beachheads, and one R–4 was for the combat engineer platoon attached to each BLT. All were waterproofed under the guidance of the 13th Engineer Combat Battalion, 7th Division, which had landed at Attu. The engineers also brought one 10,000-gallon and five trailer-mounted 2,000-gallon units for distilling water, and three paving smashers for excavating in coral.

The divisional G–4 staff section had previously formulated, for whatever overseas mission might require embarkation of the entire division, a careful table of supply requirements and their cubic content, and a loading plan with orders of priority. These data proved useful in the highly complicated task of loading and stowing cargo for the expedition. The Task Force commander, Admiral Turner, insisted that the cargo be stowed in such a fashion that the load be evenly balanced in each ship. The 27th Division staff was primarily interested in combat loading, an arrangement which would link matériel with personnel, ship for ship, each vessel carrying what its occupants would need in battle, and at the same time would load it in layers of relative urgency, so that the lowest would be the least necessary rather than the heaviest. The requirements of seaworthiness and navigability clashed in some degree with those of maximum efficiency in supporting land combat. Adjusting these conflicting requirements was difficult, but was accomplished by altering the plans to which Admiral Turner objected without departing from the combat-loading principle.

Another logistics problem was met by pallet loading, a practice which had been tried at Attu with inconclusive results. To make possible the unloading and removal of supplies with a minimum of delay while under enemy fire, and to achieve some other lesser advantages, the 27th Division adopted the pallet system for the Makin operation.[1] Pallet loading is prodigal of cargo space, and in the Gilberts expedition, left unused about 46 percent of the basic ship tonnage capacity. Naval officers at Oahu were understandably opposed to a practice which seemed so wasteful.

---

[1] Pallets are large units of supplies or ammunition which can be hoisted or lowered in slings, kept intact while on shipboard or in small craft, and dragged ashore. The packages are fastened together and to a sled- or toboggan-like base by metal straps.

In favor of pallet loading, however, was not only the reduced exposure to enemy fire for those unloading at the beaches, but also the smaller number of men needed to do the unloading. A larger proportion therefore was free for combat. Although cargo space went unused, of the cargo which was brought ashore, much less was wasted because the sleds kept perishables above the mud and water and permitted the drawing of cargo units swiftly to the supply dumps. (See illustration, p. 19.) Ammunition handling and rehandling could also be curtailed. In the end, in consultation with a naval officer who had made a special investigation, 1,850 4' x 6' pallets of two types were adopted.

Each BLT was to be loaded on its own transport with most of its landing craft. Headquarters and other units went on a fourth APA (Transport, Attack). The radar detachment, with its heavy trailers, and various service detachments were to ride on an AKA (Cargo Vessel, Attack). Medium tanks were to be carried, with their lighters, on an LSD (Landing Ship, Dock), and 3 LST's would take the 3 special landing groups, each with its 16 Alligators. Thus nine vessels were to carry the Makin force from Oahu to the target area.

During the first week of November 1943, the final stages of planning and training reached their conclusion. The forces organized to capture Makin and develop it as an American base were gathered for embarkation. Hurried and incomplete as their preparations in some fields had necessarily been, the time had come for the expedition to move. The first aggressive drive toward Tokyo in the Central Pacific Area was about to begin.

The Assault from the
Western Beaches

The Approach

THE MAIN BODY OF THE NORTHERN ATTACK FORCE left Pearl Harbor bound for Makin during the afternoon of 10 November 1943. Its transports had arrived in time to rehearse loadings and landings with small craft; the departure was in most respects as if for another training exercise. The main body was the third portion of the force to leave Hawaii. The first was part of the garrison force in six LST's with an escorting destroyer. They had sailed on 31 October. Five days later, the three LST's bearing the valued Alligators and the special landing groups set forth with a destroyer escort, on a somewhat shorter route and at a speed which was to bring them to their destination at the same time as the main assault convoy. On 15 November two transports and three cargo vessels were to begin taking the bulk of the garrison force to Makin.

In the convoy carrying the main assault force, each of the three BLT's was assigned to a separate transport. The 3d BLT was on the *Leonard Wood,* along with Division Headquarters. The *Neville* carried the 2d, and the *Calvert* brought the 1st. Col. Gardiner J. Conroy, commander of the 165th Regiment, with some of the regimental units, the field artillery, engineer, tank, and garrison headquarters elements, and various detachments, was on the *Pierce,* a fourth transport. On the cargo vessel, *Alcyone,* were the radar group, cannon company, some service units, and some small special detachments. Smallest of the 6 transport vessels was the LSD *Belle Grove,* with 15 medium tanks and Company A, 193d Tank Battalion.

These ships were part of a mighty fleet of warships also bound for Makin. Four battleships, four cruisers, and nine aircraft carriers carried the main striking power; they were screened by ten destroyers.

Impressive as the Northern Attack Force must have seemed to the men on the transports bound for Makin, it was only part of a greater aggregation of ships and men advancing upon the Gilberts. From the New Hebrides two other carrier groups which had just participated in an air strike upon Rabaul were moving to neutralize Nauru and to support the assault upon Tarawa. For the latter, a larger convoy of marines was zigzagging through the New Hebrides to a point southeast of Funafuti. Its course was to bring it off Tarawa on a final leg parallel to that of the Northern Attack Force. Both would approach their objectives during the night of 19/20 November.

Assaults upon Makin and Tarawa were to begin at the same hour, 0830, on 20 November. Vice Adm. R. A. Spruance commanded the entire expedition, his fleet flag being on the *Indianapolis;*[1] Defense Forces and Shore-based Air Forces were under Rear Adm. J. H. Hoover; the Carrier Force, under Rear Adm. C. A. Pownall; and the Assault Forces, under Admiral Turner. With him on the *Pennsylvania* were Maj. Gen. Holland M. Smith, USMC, commanding the V Amphibious Corps, and Col. W. O. Eareckson, commanding the Support Aircraft. Admiral Turner's direct command extended also to the Northern Attack Force. The Southern Attack Force was commanded by Rear Adm. H. W. Hill.

As soon as the landing forces were established on the island, all shore-based land, sea, and air units were to fall under the command of the senior troop commander, which at Tarawa meant Maj. Gen. Julian C. Smith, USMC, and at Makin, Maj. Gen. Ralph C. Smith of the 27th Division. When capture was complete, command was to pass to designated garrison force commanders; at Makin this would be Col. C. H. Tenney.

The exact mission of the expedition was announced to the men on the transports two hours after the start. For the remaining nine days of the voyage, intelligence material was studied at the various levels from maps, sand tables, information folders, air and panoramic mosaics, and photo-interpretation charts. Squads and detachments reviewed their respective missions. Morale was excellent, the tension

---

[1] See Organization Chart, p. 32.

of the first part of the trip being broken by the merriment attending a celebration of the crossing of the equator.

The expedition approached the Gilberts, knowing that some of its elements had been discovered and reported by enemy air observers. The main transport group may have escaped attention, but the slower party consisting of three LST's and their escorting destroyer was under attack during the last two days before they reached Makin. They drove away a Japanese "Mavis" late in the afternoon of 18 November, at a time when the Southern Carrier Group was also under attack, and at 1405 on the next day they watched a 10-minute battle between three friendly planes and a Japanese "Betty" which ended when the latter was shot down. Their own turn came after dark, for then two enemy planes, a "Nell" and a "Betty," returned to the attack.

As the "Nell" swept in low over the group, guns blazed at it from every ship within range. Army gun crews even manned the heavy machine guns in an LCT which was part of the deck cargo of the LST 31. The plane began to burn as it neared the LST 31, veered in a swiftly descending glide, and, like a flaming torch, headed toward the LST 179 as if to crash upon her deck. Swooping low over her bow, the plane plunged into the ocean; burning oil lighted up the entire group of ships for several minutes. Soon afterward, the second plane departed.

In the main convoy, submarine warnings were issued after contact with an unidentified submarine which was eventually found to be the *Nautilus*. General quarters was sounded three times on the last afternoon. From the *Colorado* 12 Liberators were sighted at 1535 on their way from Nanomea to Makin, part of a bombing schedule which kept the Japanese in their shelters or manning their weak antiaircraft defenses repeatedly during the week of landing. As the expedition drew near to its goal and enemy contacts increased, it could no longer count upon surprise. The Japanese were known to have radar installations on Makin, and could also be presumed to be on general alert in normal reaction to the greatly increased air activity.

In the early hours of 20 November, the Northern Attack Force arrived at its destination. The LST's were on a somewhat different course from the remainder of the force, and radio silence made knowledge of their exact location unobtainable. The Air Support

31

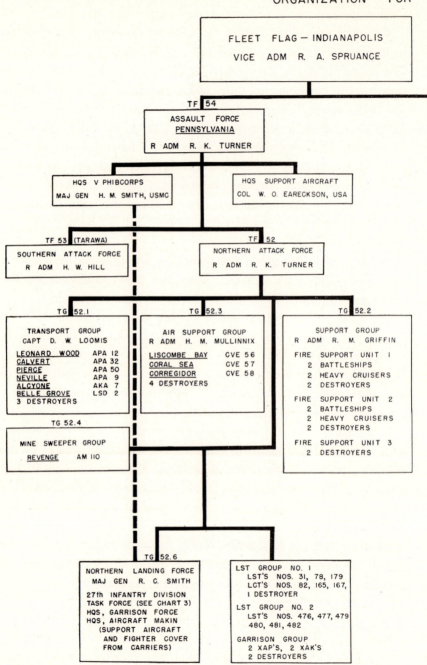

ORGANIZATION FOR

FLEET FLAG — INDIANAPOLIS
VICE ADM R. A. SPRUANCE

TF 54
ASSAULT FORCE
PENNSYLVANIA
R ADM R. K. TURNER

HQS V PHIBCORPS
MAJ GEN H. M. SMITH, USMC

HQS SUPPORT AIRCRAFT
COL W. O. EARECKSON, USA

TF 53 (TARAWA)
SOUTHERN ATTACK FORCE
R ADM H. W. HILL

TF 52
NORTHERN ATTACK FORCE
R ADM R. K. TURNER

TG 52.1
TRANSPORT GROUP
CAPT D. W. LOOMIS

LEONARD WOOD	APA 12
CALVERT	APA 32
PIERCE	APA 50
NEVILLE	APA 9
ALCYONE	AKA 7
BELLE GROVE	LSD 2
3 DESTROYERS	

TG 52.3
AIR SUPPORT GROUP
R ADM H. M. MULLINNIX

LISCOMBE BAY	CVE 56
CORAL SEA	CVE 57
CORREGIDOR	CVE 58
4 DESTROYERS	

TG 52.2
SUPPORT GROUP
R ADM R. M. GRIFFIN

FIRE SUPPORT UNIT 1
2 BATTLESHIPS
2 HEAVY CRUISERS
2 DESTROYERS

FIRE SUPPORT UNIT 2
2 BATTLESHIPS
2 HEAVY CRUISERS
2 DESTROYERS

FIRE SUPPORT UNIT 3
2 DESTROYERS

TG 52.4
MINE SWEEPER GROUP
REVENGE AM 110

TG 52.6
NORTHERN LANDING FORCE
MAJ GEN R. C. SMITH

27th INFANTRY DIVISION
TASK FORCE (SEE CHART 3)
HQS, GARRISON FORCE
HQS, AIRCRAFT MAKIN
(SUPPORT AIRCRAFT
AND FIGHTER COVER
FROM CARRIERS)

LST GROUP NO. 1
LST'S NOS. 31, 78, 179
LCT'S NOS. 82, 165, 167,
1 DESTROYER

LST GROUP NO. 2
LST'S NOS. 476, 477, 479
480, 481, 482

GARRISON GROUP
2 XAP'S, 2 XAK'S
2 DESTROYERS

CHART NO. 3

52

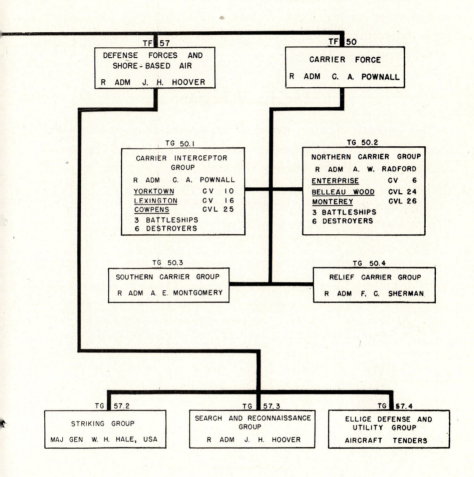

TF 57
DEFENSE FORCES AND
SHORE - BASED AIR
R ADM J. H. HOOVER

TF 50
CARRIER FORCE
R ADM C. A. POWNALL

TG 50.1
CARRIER INTERCEPTOR
GROUP
R ADM C. A. POWNALL
YORKTOWN   CV 10
LEXINGTON   CV 16
COWPENS   CVL 25
3 BATTLESHIPS
6 DESTROYERS

TG 50.2
NORTHERN CARRIER GROUP
R ADM A. W. RADFORD
ENTERPRISE   CV 6
BELLEAU WOOD   CVL 24
MONTEREY   CVL 26
3 BATTLESHIPS
6 DESTROYERS

TG 50.3
SOUTHERN CARRIER GROUP
R ADM A. E. MONTGOMERY

TG 50.4
RELIEF CARRIER GROUP
R ADM F. C. SHERMAN

TG 57.2
STRIKING GROUP
MAJ GEN W. H. HALE, USA

TG 57.3
SEARCH AND RECONNAISSANCE
GROUP
R ADM J. H. HOOVER

TG 57.4
ELLICE DEFENSE AND
UTILITY GROUP
AIRCRAFT TENDERS

Group deployed to an area about 20 miles southeast of Butaritari. The transports moved toward a designated transport area about four miles west of the island. Screening the carriers and transports, and preparing for the initial bombardment, the other warships moved closer to the shore. Between 0258 and 0600, as daylight came, no enemy fire was received and the attacking force prepared to launch its heavy blows.

The Assault Begins

The approach of dawn found all the convoy in place except the three LST's with their important load of Alligators. In case either the Alligators, or the medium tanks, or both had failed to reach Makin, alternative plans of attack were ready, but the LST's arrived at 0700 during the naval bombardment and completed the convoy. The plan of attack was able to proceed unaltered.

WESTERN BEACHES *of Butaritari as viewed by the Northern Landing Force on the transports during the preparatory naval bombardment of 20 November 1943. Shells are bursting near the two Red Beaches, and the men have already commenced their debarkation into landing barges.*

LANDING BARGES CIRCLE *in the rendezvous area off Butaritari waiting for the time to form assault waves. They are to carry part of the 1st Battalion Landing Team, 165th Infantry (reinforced), into Red Beach from the transport* Calvert. *In the distance a heavy gun flashes.*

The assault opened with air strikes from the carriers at 0617. Enemy anticraft fire was very weak. Dive-bombers bombed and strafed the beaches while glide-bombers worked over the clearing at the West Tank barrier. They dropped 74 tons of half-ton and 1-ton demolition bombs, and 1-ton "daisy-cutters."[1] The transports moved to their allotted area 6,000 yards from the beach and lowered small boats. The warships took their stations and, after the airplanes had completed their missions, opened at 0640 a systematic bombardment of the entire area of the day's assigned ground operations. It was to continue for almost four hours.

At 0645, two LCVP's (Landing Craft, Vehicle, Personnel) left the side of the *Neville.* They carried a special detachment consisting

---

[1] The commanding officer of the garrison was killed, according to a prisoner of war, Cpl. Toshimitsu Saito, interviewed on 4 December 1943.

of 19 marines of the 4th Platoon of the v Amphibious Corps Reconnaissance Company, under 1st Lt. Harvey C. Weeks, USMCR, and the reinforced 2d Platoon, Company G, 2d BLT, under 2d Lt. Earl W. Montgomery. They headed for Kotabu Island, a small, round island about four miles away, and less than a mile and a half north of Flink Point. Naval bombardment preceded them as they plunged into the ground swell on a ride of almost an hour.

The strafing of the planes had raised one inverted cone of black smoke from a fire north of Red Beach 1. The naval bombardment raised such a pall of smoke and dust as to obscure the island completely from the transports. And then came a sudden, drenching squall from the south, which eventually cleared the air over the island and restored visibility. Reconnaissance planes reported conditions favorable for landings, with waves no higher than three feet. Fires in the "citadel" area and near Ukiangong Point attested the effectiveness of the naval bombardment there. But in the Red Beach areas it had been less damaging than the attackers desired, much of it either falling short or exploding among the coconut and pandanus trees some distance in from the beach.

Debarkation of the 1st BLT from the *Calvert,* and of the 3d BLT from the *Leonard Wood,* began with the lowering of landing craft from both sides of the transports as soon as they stopped in the transport area at 0600. Soon the boats moved to the rendezvous area. (See illustration, p. 35.) At 0758, they started breaking away from the circling group to form the first wave of each BLT at the line of departure, which was marked by the destroyers, *Phelps* and *MacDonough,* 2,800 yards offshore. The two destroyers moved in, pumping 5-inch shells into the boundary zone at the inner edge of the beaches as the bigger guns of the battleships and cruisers fell temporarily silent. From the LST's two "V's" of Alligators led the way in. The first waves of landing craft crossed the line of departure at 0818 with a further run of 14 minutes to the beach. Three minutes ahead of them were the Alligators; five minutes behind came the second and later waves. Even the third wave for each beach was therefore en route when the first arrived at the end of the run.

The first wave of the 1st BLT going to Red Beach 1 contained 233 men in 7 boats; the next 4 waves were somewhat smaller, consisting of six boats only. The landing craft in each wave formed two wide triangles; four LCM's (Landing Craft, Mechanized) carrying

36

tanks were in front and on the two wings; two LCVP's occupied the inner positions. The seventh boat in the first wave was an LCVP at the rear center in which rode the battalion and Company D commanders, the air-ground and navy liaison parties, and communications personnel.

Each of the four LCM's was expected to bring ashore a light tank (M3A1) with its crew, one light machine-gun squad, two rifle squads, several noncommissioned officers, messengers, and a company aid man. Each of the LCVP's took in a 60-mm mortar squad and 2 rifle squads, platoon and section guides and leaders, and individual specialists, a boatload totaling 33 men.

On the right of this first assault wave of the 1st BLT, heading toward Red Beach 2, was the corresponding wave of the 3d BLT, following a similar schedule of debarkations and landings. Thus, had all plans been executed without mishap, over 460 men and 8 tanks would have moved up the western shore of Butaritari at 0832, following the Alligators across the two separated beach areas.

When the men of the 1st and 3d BLT's started in toward the two Red Beaches, they could see before them a flat strip of shore and skyline stretching over 5,000 yards from point to point. Light showed under the tops of the coconut palms on either point, but elsewhere the vegetation indicated no clearings free of underbrush. The landmarks were not prominent. Dips in the treeline, bushes growing in clumps close to the water's edge, huts near the beach, and patches of dark boulders which interrupted the gleaming white of the beach furnished the few points of reference. Bobbing about in little boats in the rendezvous area, soaked by rain and spray after standing since dawn on the decks of the *Calvert* and the *Leonard Wood,* the men got a general impression of a low, flat, tree-covered island. Closer approach from the line of departure sharpened the details; the blurred smoothness of the left half of Red Beach 1 gave way to the roughness of a boulder-strewn slope, short and rocky. The right half was seen to be no beach at all but a bulge into the ocean closely studded with boulders.

The craft carrying the 1st BLT to Red Beach took them to its left half, keeping to the left of a large bush, almost a haystack in proportions, near the water and in front of four very high coconut palms. Those going to Red Beach 2 diverged toward another landmark, the northernmost of several native huts, about 1,100 yards to the

RED BEACH TWO *was sandy, smooth, gently sloping, yet wide enough for only three barges at once until improved by troops of the 152d Engineers. Adjacent terrain was ideal for supply dumps. Here the 3d BLT landed, and early on D Day, 105th Field Artillery guns came in.*

right of the 1st BLT landings. Centering on this hut, they found about 75 yards of reasonably smooth, stony beach to which access was readily made at high tide. The beach rose gradually over coral stones to firm and fairly level ground, shaded by a coconut grove and occupied by a native hamlet.

The Alligators approached the beaches firing upon the zone of possible enemy activity. Rocket volleys fell short at first, and then were only partly successful; rain and spray made the firing mechanism on several LVT's useless. At 1,000 yards their .50-cal. machine guns opened up; 200 yards farther in they were joined by the .30-cal. machine guns. As they came closer to Red Beach 2, return fire coming from rifles rather than from the mounted guns believed to be emplaced behind the southern half of that beach wounded one seaman and killed another. About 100 yards offshore, the amphibians came over the coral reef. No barbed wire, mines, or other military obstacles impeded them. At 0829, as their tracks began to touch the rocks, like clumsy, bizarre reptiles they scraped their way forward, somehow lumbered up the shoulders of the beach, and perched on boulders which held them high in the air. Over the sides, the heavily-loaded men of the special detachments scrambled and dropped to seek cover. Many stood, however, waiting first for enemy fire before taking precautions. The special detachments moved to the right and left extremities of the beaches and mounted defensive flank positions. From the upper edge of the shore, on Red Beach 2, they replied to weak sniping from the woods for about five minutes, and when it ceased they moved on to the right.

TROOPS ON RED BEACH ONE *among the jagged boulders await the signal to advance. At their right, a light tank of the 193d Tank Battalion, which came ashore in the first assault wave, moves south along the beach, having first ground its way over the rocks in foreground.*

Landings on Red Beach 1 did not, unfortunately, proceed on schedule. A hoist on the *Calvert* was disabled before the fourth tank was unloaded. The first wave therefore had but three tanks. The Alligators, tank lighters, and landing craft finished the journey on a course almost parallel to the swell, rising and falling about three feet as they drew near to the beach. The intervening reef was studded with coral boulders, rough and jagged lumps as much as two feet high, which left no passage from the edge of the reef, about 100 yards out, to high water mark. Coming in on a rising tide, the several landing craft were unable to make the simultaneous touchdowns provided by the plans. Some slipped past most of the boulders and were held less than a boat's length (36 feet) from the water's edge, but many were broached, stranded, or forced to put to sea again. The tanks had been waterproofed for the landing, and rolled off the ramps into water which did not quite drown them out, but ahead of them the men struggled in swells breast deep, stumbled over the rocks and boulders, or sought cover at the edge of the beach.

Red Beach 1 was itself very rough above the waterline; it was usable for only 15 yards of width and rose swiftly from high tide mark to vegetation. Far from taking all six craft in each of the waves, it could not take more than three abreast near the shoreline, while for unloading supplies efficiently from even one boat, a channel had to be blasted. The first barges found great difficulty in withdrawing to give room for later assault waves to land. The Army officer in charge of the Alligators declined to divert them from their original inland assignments and put them to pulling stranded boats off the rocks, but the Navy furnished a crew which operated one LVT in that service. The absence of enemy opposition to the landings at Red Beach 1 made it possible to meet the adverse beach conditions without suffering casualties.

The carefully prepared sequence in the arrival of various elements of the assault and shore parties was thrown into confusion by the conditions arising at Red Beach 1. Although the assault forces of the first five waves got ashore and moved inland, or took up their duties at the shore, the fifth wave which had been scheduled to land at 0857 actually completed its assignment at 1003. After the second wave had pushed in among the obstructions and reached the beach, the next three waves became intermingled. It had been planned to land a tractor in the second wave, to pull to cover across the open beach the palletized material landing later. While heavy machine-gun and mortar squads, and the reserve forces of Company A, came in, the shore party was to be built up by the successive arrival of its radio, command, reconnaissance, map, message center, medical, engineer, liaison, security, and naval boat control elements. Other communications material and personnel were to arrive in the fourth and fifth waves, and in the latter, four 37-mm guns with their crews and tractors. Actually it proved impossible to land jeeps and their trailers, and before long LVT's were acting as ferries, transferring cargo from the boats at the edge of the reef to the beach.

From the transport *Calvert,* 913 officers and enlisted men, and 81¾ tons of equipment were dispatched on D Day, and while the men were landed with some of the equipment, much of the latter was still afloat in the landing barges at nightfall.

The approach to Red Beach 2 was somewhat freer of impediments than that to Red Beach 1 but it was far from clear. The 3d BLT of 1,250 men was scheduled to land there in seven assault waves at 5-minute intervals beginning at 0832. Actually, beginning at 0840 the first three waves landed as such, but the remaining boats landed singly. It was 1022 before the seventh wave arrived off the beach. During D Day the *Leonard Wood* sent ashore 1,250 men, 4 tanks, 1 bulldozer, 5 jeeps, and 4 antitank guns. Light and ineffective enemy machine-gun fire was reported by several wave commanders.

The 1st BLT Advances

The inland advance from the Red Beaches proceeded so closely in accordance with the plans that it was conducted mainly under direction of officers of company grade. Colonel Conroy and other field officers were chiefly concerned with supply, communications, and intelligence. The major difficulties encountered by the infantry of the 1st and 3d BLT's came from the terrain.

Although the two teams moved forward simultaneously, the chief improved roads, important sites for American supply installations, and the artillery positions were in the sector occupied by the 3d BLT on the right (Map No. 5, p. 14). The other area had little military importance except as a beachhead. Flink Point was topographically unsuitable for either artillery positions or supply installations; it was separated from the rest of the island by a water passage into the lagoon which ran through one of its three large areas of marsh and mangrove. The greater part of the zone at the left consisted of mangrove swamp, shallow lakes, and marshy, brush-covered terrain with trails few or poor, and only one small native hamlet north of Red Beach 1. The almost unopposed advance of the 1st BLT to the beachhead line was, in effect, a mere preliminary to its more important role in the second phase of the drive toward the West Tank Barrier.

As the forces of the 1st BLT accumulated on Red Beach 1, they organized at the top of the beach and advanced upon their several missions. The Alligators could not overcome the obstacles to lateral movement along the beach; they therefore moved onto the sandy soil above the beach and struggled through trees and debris to a flank position and to the long narrow point beyond it. The 132 men of Special Detachment Y left one platoon at the flank and continued along the point in search of enemy forces. Their progress was slow, and long before they reached the tip, they had been able to see the barges start for the Yellow Beach landings and to notice the smoke rising from fires near that beach. The main force of the 1st BLT moved forward toward the beachhead line about 1,300 yards ahead to the east.

They met insignificant sniper fire only; their main difficulty came from the debris and the watery holes resulting from the air and naval bombardment. (See illustrations, opposite.) Great masses of tough, closely matted root fibers barred their way. Working through them and through the other obstacles, the men found that preserving contact required constant attention. While taking care not to lose contact, they also watched constantly for snipers, whose fire was random and inaccurate. It was the first experience of enemy fire for the battalion.

Light tanks could not make headway against the combined obstacles of debris, shell holes, and marsh except by remaining on the roads. Those which landed with the 1st BLT were initially held up by their refusal to receive commands except through their own company officers, and then by the difficulties of terrain. Although they came in before 0900, they were of no assistance to the infantry of the 1st BLT until late in the day, at 1430. A naval shell which struck the main highway in the swampy area created such an obstacle that the whole tank group was held up until midafternoon.

TERRAIN TORN UP *by preparatory bombardment is encountered be-hind Red Beaches by the 1st and 3d BLT's. They advance with difficulty. (Below) A sniper's shot has just electrified these men, who are taking cover and looking for the position from which the enemy has fired.*

The 1st BLT advanced with three companies abreast. At the right Company B and some of the 1st Platoon (Heavy Machine Gun), Company D, covered the widest zone; their first action was the seizure of an observation tower, protected by barbed wire and log barricades, but not defended. In the center Company C moved straight ahead without waiting for the heavily laden 2d Platoon (Heavy Machine Gun) of Company D to emerge from the water and assemble its weapons. Company A remained at first in dispersed formation as battalion reserve, along with uncommitted portions of Company D, but absence of serious enemy resistance permitted it to start inland at 0900 and to take a more advanced position from which to be available as reserve.

At the end of the first phase Company B and Company C held the left half of the beachhead line just east of "Rita Lake," and were in contact with Company K of the 3d BLT just across the island highway on the right flank. In fulfillment of the plans the 1st BLT then extended its line to cross the entire island, relieving the 3d BLT so that it might go into reserve. Patrols were sent forward as far as "Jill Lake" to locate enemy positions in preparation for a later advance (Map No. 5, p. 14). The main body of the 1st BLT waited for the end of the naval bombardment of areas adjacent to Yellow Beach; at about 1100 it started forward again.

The 3d BLT Advances

The ineffective Japanese opposition to the landings on Red Beach 2 ceased in less than ten minutes. Special Detachment X swung to the right and established a defensive position on the southern flank. Headquarters units and Companies I, K, and L, with a detachment of light tanks, moved inland. Company K took possession of what was discovered to be a dummy battery and pushed eastward through the wooded, northern half of the battalion's sector, next to Company B of the 1st BLT. An unimproved road at the south end of the hamlet near the beach curved gradually to a junction with the main island highway, some 300 yards in from the beach. Around this road junction (RJ–4, Map No. 5, p. 14) and south of it, the invaders had been warned to expect a Japanese strongpoint. Company I moved directly upon the center, while the flanks were in the lines of advance of Company K on the left and Company L on the right. Like the dummy guns, this strongpoint proved to be unoccupied. Moving inland at the rate of 20 yards per minute, while the fifth wave came into the beach behind them, the men of the 3d BLT passed a few deserted huts and came without untoward incident to the main highway.

The area traversed by the 3d BLT on its way to the beachhead line was the counterpart, in general, of that confronting the 1st BLT at the same time. But it contained three of the four suspected Japanese strongpoints, a considerable native village (Ukiangong), and the site intended for the American artillery. As Company K

A FLANK PATROL on Red Beach One is swiftly established by one of three special landing detachments formed for such missions from the 105th Infantry. These troops were the first ashore, being carried by groups of 16 LVT's (Alligators) ahead of waves of infantry with tanks.

moved almost straight eastward, Company I fanned out in a triangular area between the main highway and the ocean south of Company K's territory, and Company L, assisted by part of Special Detachment X, turned south to take Ukiangong village and to clear the whole point beyond it.

One platoon of Company L moved parallel to the western shore, a short distance inland. The rest of the company, with the light tank platoon, advanced upon the 40 or 50 thatch-roofed huts which, strung along the coral-surfaced highway, and bounded on the west by irregular patches of coconut grove and *bobai* pits, constituted the village. They had been warned to expect the harsh welcome of ten Japanese machine guns. No opposition whatever was encountered.

About an hour after moving inland, left flank elements of Company K reached the western extremity of "Rita Lake," the largest of several shallow ponds. The eastern edge of that pond stretched almost the entire length of the beachhead line south of the point at which it was crossed by the island highway. At a slight elevation the highway crossed the western lobe of the pond (Map No. 5, p. 14), then cut for about 300 yards through scattered growth, and finally skirted the pond's northern shore for a similar distance.

Patrols from Company K probed along this highway and combed the woods between the southern edge of "Rita Lake" and the ocean shore. At last, two hours after the first landing, one of these units had the first fire fight of the day with a group of the enemy, and killed five of them. At 1055 the line was reached; Company K was shortly relieved by the 1st BLT in fulfillment of the tactical plan, and withdrew to an assembly area in a coconut grove near the ocean, several hundred yards southwest of "Rita Lake."

On Ukiangong Point, Company L and its associated units overran one supposedly critical area after another, without resistance. What had been thought to be defense installations proved instead to be a stone-crushing plant, two large dummy guns, some neat square piles of coral rock, and some bomb shelters. Having pressed their search throughout the area, this unit of the 3d BLT rejoined the battalion in the coconut grove later in the day. There during the afternoon they established a perimeter defense and settled down for the night. Since it was possible that they might be needed at Tarawa, they were kept in position and were not recommitted on Makin for about 36 hours.

Conditions at the Beaches

Arrangements to reinforce and to supply the advancing BLT's began in the wake of the early waves of the attack. The first five assault waves also brought elements of the shore parties, which eventually reached totals of approximately 250 men. Ship-to-shore communications teams from the 27th and 75th Signal Company Detachments set up radios in the shelter of the coconut trees a few yards in from the shore itself. Radio nets and wire lines, which were laid hastily on the ground, were established by the Communications Platoon, 165th Infantry, and the signal company detachments to link the two beaches with each other and with the CP's as soon as they should be set up. Shore Fire Control Party teams and air-ground liaison teams found positions for their radios. The engineers organized teams to unload the boats, as well as others to maintain communications and liaison with other elements of the landing force. The beachmaster and his navy units prepared to survey the approaches to the beaches, to make maps, to repair boats, and to maintain communications and medical service.

Against possible enemy air attack, batteries of the 93d Coast Artillery (AA) (less their 2d Platoons) prepared positions near the flank defenses on each Red Beach, but could not set up their guns until the next day. For close-in protection the security detachments of Company B, 152d Engineers, were used.

Fire support of the troops was also prepared by a reconnaissance party of the 105th Field Artillery, which came ashore in the fourth wave. It made its way with Company L to Ukiangong village, and verified the suitability of an area south of the village for the emplacement of the battalion's twelve 105-mm guns. At 1100 the guns were brought ashore, with tractors and heavy trucks for ammunition. In less than three hours they would be ready to fire.

The terrain in the rear of Red Beach 2 was convenient and suitable for supply dumps. During the morning of D Day, ammunition, signal and medical supplies, water in cans, and ordnance repair facilities were established in the area. Rations were also stored near Red Beach 1. Medical aid stations were put into operation on each beach, but seriously wounded men were sent out to the ships for treatment on the first day; it had not been possible to land the clearing station matériel in its three 2½-ton trucks.

INFANTRY MOVES ALONG MAIN ISLAND HIGHWAY *toward the West Tank Barrier. Hastily unreeled signal wire lies on the road.*

Although the enemy offered no resistance to the steps taken to support and supply the attacking troops, the difficult off-shore landing conditions interfered seriously with the plans. These conditions first curtailed the use of Red Beach 1 and forced the diversion at 1300 of some boats to Red Beach 2. At 1030 the latter was operating satisfactorily but Red Beach 1 was able to handle only one small boat at a time. The divisional G–4, Lt. Col. Charles B. Ferris, discovered a beach about 300 yards nearer Flink Point which was itself satisfactory, and the approach to which could be made adequate by blasting coral pinnacles and boulders on the reef. He so reported. By midafternoon, as the tide went down, Red Beach 2 was also the scene of congested boat traffic. Landing craft were stranded so thoroughly that it took the combined efforts of a bulldozer and an amphibian tractor to slide them into deeper water. No boats were sent to the Red Beaches after 1700, and those as yet unloaded were then ordered into the lagoon for the night.

From the *Calvert,* approximately one-tenth of the scheduled landings of supplies and equipment upon Red Beach 1 had been possible during the entire day.

Early in the course of the landings, natives of Makin began emerging from their hiding places in the brush; at first a chief and soon scores of all ages appeared on Red Beach 1. Some of the adults seemed to be still stunned by the bombardment, but the preliminary action had had surprisingly little effect and losses were taken calmly by the survivors. They acted as if pleased by the advent of the Americans, swarmed aboard the Alligators, and seemed fascinated by the modern weapons of war. To interrogators they declared that about 400 enemy soldiers, 450 workers, and 2 tanks comprised the Japanese strength on Butaritari. This report was sent to the *Leonard Wood* at 1040. Half an hour later another group was interrogated on Red Beach 2, and a report sent to General Ralph C. Smith that they estimated the enemy strength to be 500 men, with 6 large-caliber guns.

The Japanese had denied water to the natives for three days prior to the attack. American troops shared some of the water which they brought ashore and gave them K rations.

Ukiangong village was now deserted but the small village on Red Beach 2 remained occupied by the natives until they were moved out near a source of fresh water on Flink Point, where they would not get in the way of the work with equipment and supplies. About 480 natives finally congregated at the point and, except for a labor force, were kept there by a staff of military police.

Enemy documents were found and sent out to Admiral Turner early in the afternoon. They had been left behind in a hasty departure from the shelter near the lookout tower, at the point between the two Red Beaches. Two prisoners were also taken, who reported their belief that a Japanese relief expedition consisting of two task forces was coming.

Before the end of the morning, each of the BLT's and the regiment had set up CP's, while Division Headquarters had an advanced station ashore. Lt. Col. Gerard W. Kelley's post in command of the 1st BLT was then near RJ–1 (Map No. 5, p. 14), while that of Lt. Col. Joseph T. Hart was near RJ–5. After the beachhead line had been reached, Colonel Conroy took over regimental command from a station near RJ–4. The advance post of the 27th Division Headquarters was on a trail about 50 yards inland from Red Beach 2 and 100 yards south of RJ–4.

As the 1st BLT resumed its advance toward the West Tank Barrier at about 1100 and the 2d BLT came ashore through the lagoon, the supply lines on the western beaches were being strengthened, and communications teams were struggling to link CP's with advance elements and with headquarters afloat. The artillery was being sent ashore. The main battle seemed about to begin.

WESTERN HALF OF YELLOW BEACH AREA *at dawn of D Day, as seen from a Navy spotting plane. At right West Tank Barrier, goal of first day's operations, and hulks from which men in barges in the lagoon believed that they received enemy fire. On Chong's Wharf is in center.*

Taking the West Tank Barrier

Landings at Yellow Beach

WHEN THE LANDINGS ON THE RED BEACHES were known to be progressing without significant opposition, the 2d BLT at 0856 moved to the second transport area, west of Kotabu Island. The *Neville,* with its boats already lowered, the LSD *Belle Grove,* and the LST *179* carried the troops, tanks, and Alligators for Yellow Beach. The *Belle Grove* launched the LCM's carrying medium tanks (and two LCVP's) between 0910 and 0923. The LST *179* continued to the third transport area within the lagoon and there launched the 16 Alligators which carried Special Detachment Z of the 105th Infantry; they faced the most hazardous mission of the Yellow Beach landing force. Behind them the landing craft formed waves, started passing through the channel between Flink Point and Kotabu Island at 0952, and crossed the line of departure at 1012. From there to the beach the course ran east-southeast for about 6,000 yards, bringing them into the area between On Chong's Wharf and King's Wharf after a run of 18 minutes.

YELLOW BEACH UNDER ATTACK
*at 1045 on D Day. Smoke pours up from
four burning fuel dumps, one in center of
beach. While barges are caught on reef,
Alligators have gone ashore, leaving muddy trails, and tanks have begun to follow
them. On Chong's Wharf is seen at left.*

The naval bombardment, fluctuating in violence since 0720, grew noticeably heavier at 0930 and began once more to sweep the main defensive area. Smoke soon rose from several fires among the warehouses, barracks, and other structures, and was visible through the trees to some of the units advancing overland from the west.

Using 11 landing craft from the *Alcyone* and 24 which had been brought on the *Neville*, the 2d BLT made its way toward Yellow Beach against a smooth ground swell. Companies E, F, and part of G, and Heavy Weapons Company H of the 165th Infantry, one platoon of Company C, 102d Engineers, some medical detachments, and the Yellow Beach Shore Party were disembarked by the *Neville*. From the *Belle Grove* came Company A, 193d Tank Battalion, with their medium tanks (M3), part of Battery A, and the headquarters detachments of the 98th Coast Artillery (AA). Besides the Alligators and their occupants, the LST *179* sent in the headquarters section of 193d Tank Battalion (light tanks) and two antiaircraft detachments (Battery D and part of Battery A, 98th Coast Artillery (AA)).

The movement of the first assault waves to the line of departure was watched by the landing detachment of marines and infantry on Kotabu Island. They had waded ashore in waist-deep water at 0742, crossed the beach, and taken possession of an empty island. With the first part of their mission accomplished, they waited on Kotabu for orders to move to another islet, and as they watched the preparations for the Yellow Beach landings, they had time also to recover from the strafing of a "friendly" seaplane.

The scene confronting the landing forces as they moved toward Yellow Beach was far from beautiful. A brilliant mid-morning sun poured down, intensifying the blue and green of the water and throwing Butaritari Island in shadow, but the renewed bombardment was raising banks of grayish smoke and dust over which swirled billows of thick, black smoke from fuel stores on the shore between the wharves and in the area behind King's Wharf. The light wind carried plumes of smoke over the tree tops for thousands of feet

CAUSEWAY OF KING'S WHARF, *on the left flank of Yellow Beach. Along the causeway below the line of fire from Japanese guns emplaced on it, a squad of Company M, 105th Infantry, crawled ashore after disembarking from an Alligator on the seaplane ramp at outer end.*

toward the west. It raised a few whitecaps among the choppy waves formed by the backing of low swells from the ocean into the lagoon.

Over the heads of the landing craft, the destroyers *Phelps* and *MacDonough* began pumping 720 rounds of rapid 5-inch fire at 1015, aiming at the most important targets remaining. Soon they had completely severed the base of On Chong's Wharf from the wharf itself, and had further shattered the buildings there. They threw a punishing fire upon the West Tank Barrier, on King's Wharf, on the beach between the wharves, the roadside areas inland from the beach, and finally, the area just east of King's Wharf with its defiant Japanese signal tower.

Observers from the lagoon shore in the area occupied by the 1st BLT, and others in the constantly cruising air-coordination "clippers" overhead, watched and reported the progress of the Yellow Beach assault. At 1020 the Alligators were halfway across the lagoon, with more than 3,000 yards to go. About 900 yards behind them, the tank lighters of the second wave bunted their way in an irregular line, traveling along 200 yards apart and piling several feet of spray against their blunt, sloping bows. After another 900-yard interval, the seven smaller landing craft of the third wave advanced with the first elements of two rifle companies, Company F on the right toward Butaritari, and Company E on the left. Approximately the same distance behind them were the landing boats with the remaining platoons of these two companies. The LCT and LCM of the fifth wave, which included most of Company G, were bobbing around just east of the reef which forms the lagoon's western barrier. The sixth wave, consisting chiefly of Company H, was off Flink Point and about to enter the passage through the reefs.

The men approached Yellow Beach in a gay and confident mood. Many were inattentive to the tumult; some even slept. The Alligators launched rockets in an attempted area barrage when at a distance of 1,100 yards from the shore. Three minutes earlier, the naval bombardment had ceased; the planes then roared in to take up the last phase of the preparatory strike. They first strafed the beach, then bombed and strafed progressively further inland, according to a plan which required breaking off their action when the boats were 100 yards from the beach. Fearful of running under the planes, the first wave slowed down and waited unnecessarily for a few minutes. The later waves, unlike those which had approached Red Beach 1 two hours earlier, also slowed down and kept their intervals when the first wave was thus impeded, although the medium tanks shortened the space between them and the Alligators before they stopped. The entire schedule was thus set back 12 minutes but the greater evil of congestion was avoided.

When 500 yards offshore, the invaders came under fire from machine guns in an unidentified position at the right of the axis of approach. Two steel hulks, sunk in shallow water, lay a little farther out from shore than the tip of On Chong's Wharf, and about 100 yards west of it. Also moored off the end of that wharf was a small green and white patrol boat. The fire could be coming from the wharf itself, from the hulks, from the patrol boat, or even from the island. From King's Wharf, also, or from the area at its base, bullets from machine guns and possibly from automatic rifles hit the unarmored Alligators. The seaplane ramp at the end of that pier was approximately 100 yards east of the first wave's left flank. A cross-fire of bullets whizzed over the heads of the men lying on the floors of the Alligators as, 50 yards apart, they splashed over the shallow water of the reef for the last 250 to 300 yards to the beach. The touchdown was at 1041.

One of the Alligators ran up the seaplane ramp on King's Wharf to discharge its passengers, who made their way inland by crawling along the rough western slope of the causeway out of range of the fire which swept over its top. (See illustration, p. 55.) Another developed a defective steering device and landed to the right (west) of On Chong's Wharf, so that its men dismounted there and worked their way to the left. The other Alligators swept up the beach. Three entered the cove east of the sandspit and swerved to the left; a fourth landed on the tip of the sandspit, wandered alone among the trees and ruined buildings, and likewise swung to the left; and another swung across the base of the sandspit from its western edge to join those gathering on the left flank of Yellow Beach. One Alligator went completely out of control and continued across the island toward the ocean through the heart of the Japanese defenses. It stopped only when it hit a shell crater so large that it came to a jolting halt, nose up. Japanese rifle and machine-gun fire killed two men while others successfully took cover outside. The remaining nine Alligators crawled up the beach to the shoulder and stopped for the men of the two details of Special Detachment Z to jump down and hurry to the flanks. Shell fire struck 2 of these vehicles, and among the dismounting men 5 were killed and 12 wounded during this part of the action.

The two details moved to accomplish their missions of clearing the enemy from the two wharves (On Chong's and King's), and of constructing defensive beach blocks from the base of each wharf to a point 100 yards inland, beyond the highway. On Chong's Wharf, although beaten to kindling wood (see illustration, p. 58), offered cover for the enemy, and must be seized at once. Moving by squads, the detail at the right swung forward against light opposition, pivoting on the base of the wharf, and carried out their mission. The

TERRAIN NEAR THE WEST TANK BARRIER. *Base of On Chong's Wharf in the foreground. Northern end of tank trap clearing (A) and an antitank gun emplacement (B) are at the right. In the background are Ukiangong Point (U) and three warships ready to give fire support (C).*

STORMING YELLOW BEACH, *first wave of the 2d Battalion Landing Team, 165th Infantry, wades over wide reef under machine-gun fire from wharf on each flank. At 1040, 20 November 1943, they approach the main defensive area from the lagoon. Fires from hits by big naval guns.*

men of the left force were dropped along the shore of the cove, at the base of the sandspit, and along King's Wharf. Those ashore formed a line and moved against "no great opposition" toward their goal, joining the elements coming in along the causeway. Between the two details, Alligators on the beach fired at supposed sources of enemy resistance.

Only 100 yards behind the Alligators, the tank lighters with the medium tanks came to the reef and let down their ramps. As the tanks rolled forward through shallow water some advanced successfully, but two wallowed into shell holes hidden by muddy water and were drowned out. Machine-gun fire peppered them when the crews sought to emerge. In one of them, Capt. Robert S. Brown, who commanded the medium tanks, was thus kept out of the action at a critical phase. The others squirmed across the reef, opened fire with their 37-mm guns, and one of them, at least, knocked out a machine gun which had been firing upon it from the right flank. The Alligators ahead of them may also have suffered some damage from the tank fire.

One of the mediums drove just to the left of the fuel dump, which was in flames at the center of the beach; its occupants saw an Alligator ahead blaze up as a grenade exploded in it, and barely escaped destruction themselves from one of the few land mines found on the island, which exploded at the left and shook them badly. "Then I went into a *taro* (*bobai*) pit and hung on a stump," the tank's operator later stated. "I fired about 100 rounds with the .30 at a bunch of Japs running west on the ocean side; hung up as we were, no other gun could be brought to bear." Another tank attacked a machine-gun nest on King's Wharf. The remaining tanks hesitated at the center of the beach awaiting orders, but with their commander marooned in an offshore shell hole with the communication system of the tank drowned out, no orders came through.

SECOND WAVE APPROACHING YELLOW BEACH. *A mortar crew wading through murky water carrying heavy packs. Some men step into hidden underwater shell holes and are submerged. Weapons and equipment suffer; some are lost. Troops can see the beach 200 yards ahead.*

The landing barges in the third and fourth waves swept across the lagoon through enemy fire from small arms and machine guns which struck them well out in the lagoon, with about five minutes more to go. Bullets penetrated the LCV's (Landing Craft, Vehicle), wounding a few men, but not the LCM's. When they reached the edge of the reef, the infantry learned abruptly that, in spite of the correct calculation which brought them in near the time of highest tide (1130 hours), miscalculation of the depth of the water meant that even at full tide their small boats would hit the bottom. More than 250 yards out, under enemy fire, they would have to clamber over the side and carry everything in. For such a situation no one had been prepared; officers and men alike were surprised. All hesitated for a moment; then with general realization that they must get ashore rapidly, all went over the sides with equipment in their hands and on their backs.

The intensity of enemy fire increased. Some of the men crouched; others tried vainly to run; but most of them strode forward upright. (See illustration, p. 60.) Struggling forward in water sometimes knee deep, sometimes up to chest or chin, and often stumbling into underwater shell holes, the men could make no speed. Radios, flame throwers, bazookas, and other equipment became soaked or lost. Although the men were rather closely bunched in the water, they escaped with surprisingly few casualties. Only three were killed. At the beach the men of Companies E and F divided. Just as they reached dry shore, at about 1053, a pile of gasoline drums went up with a terrific explosion, raining metal fragments over a wide area of the lagoon. The men hesitated, then rushed across a 15-yard strip of sand and hit the dirt where the vegetation of the upper beach afforded a little cover. There they waited while Alligators and tanks cleared the beach to the flanks and enemy fire diminished. Behind them, two minutes later, the fourth wave infantrymen had an experience very similar to theirs.

Red smoke grenades on the reef and panels on shore were set out to reveal the position of the troops. Out on the flanks, troops wore

squares of target cloth on their backs with "X's" painted in blue, so as to be readily spotted from friendly aircraft. At 1058 both an air coordination clipper and the air-liaison team with the 3d BLT reported that the landings on Yellow Beach were in progress. The sixth wave brought in Company H, which carried its heavy weapons ashore with less difficulty than Company D had experienced at Red Beach 1.

Boat No. 17 from the *Neville* acted as Salvage Boat for Yellow Beach. It carried Ens. Andrew P. McConnell, Jr., the assistant boat group commander, and the salvage officer, Boatswain Joseph V. Kaspar, who steered the craft as leader of the second wave. Soon after the third wave had landed, he noticed a deadly stream of fire coming from the hulks. His crew mounted three of the boat's guns on the starboard side and headed for the hulks at such an angle as to permit all guns to fire. Until one gun had jammed and the cross-fire from the beach made retirement necessary, they moved against the enemy position. Boatswain Kaspar was fatally wounded by fire from one of the old derelicts.

Landings on Yellow Beach by later waves were interrupted by an attempt to blast the two hulks in the lagoon before more damage could be inflicted by the flanking fire which seemed to come from their neighborhood. The air component ordered delay in the landings while, from 1125 to 1250, planes from the *Enterprise, Coral Sea, Corregidor,* and *Liscombe Bay* bombed and strafed the hulks. From 1150 to 1207 they were also the target of the naval guns on the destroyer *Dewey,* firing from about 5,000 yards. In such close quarters, firing upon the hulks endangered American forces approaching the beach or near the hulks on shore. Some of the destroyer's shells hit the old ships and inflicted observable damage, but others passed over the heads of Detachment Z and landed among assault waves of the 2d BLT as they pushed across the island toward the ocean and swung against the West Tank Barrier. Medical aid men who were needed ashore, and Maj. Dennis D. Claire, who was to command the forces moving to the left from Yellow Beach, were in landing craft waiting to go in. At 1239, the battalion air-liaison party requested the prompt conclusion of the shelling of the hulks in order that the "medics" might get in to those who urgently needed them. By 1253, the air-liaison party requested discontinuance at once.

The assaulting troops had penetrated the main defensive area and executed much of their tactical plan by the time these waiting landing barges had come to the reef. The tide had also begun to recede.

The Mission of the 2d BLT

Orders for the advance inland from the lagoon provided for a swift movement southward across the island, by which the West Tank Barrier would be cut off from the remainder of the citadel area. The left wing was then expected to hold while the right made "its main effort to the west to effect contact with RCT 165." Company E and assisting units were to form a line across the island which would face east and advance about 600 yards to the road running across the island from the base of King's Wharf. Company F was to execute a similar movement to the right with the support of the larger part of Company G (less the elements which had gone to Kotabu Island with the marine detail). At the lagoon end of each line was to be a detail from the Special Detachment Z, 105th Infantry. Heavy Weapons Company H was to support the inland operations from positions near the beach. To offset the enemy's supposed greater strength in the "citadel" area, the foot soldiers had been preceded across the beach by a company of medium tanks and were to have their support during the movement inland. Early in the afternoon the West Tank Barrier would be approached from both sides as the 1st BLT also advanced from the west, supported by a platoon of light tanks. The barrier would thus fall by envelopment.

The two attacks from separate beaches were to be closely coordinated. Phase lines for the 1st BLT were expected to bring it finally to the West Tank Barrier clearing at the same time that the 2d BLT overcame the defenses on the opposite side and drove retreating Japanese westward. Careful coordination was required because of the flat terrain and the cramped space, for, as the area under enemy control narrowed, the fire of one attacking element might easily carry beyond the enemy to other attacking forces. These conditions precluded artillery or naval gunfire support. Adjustment by one BLT to departures from schedule by the other would depend upon radio communication, which the soaking of radio instruments during the landings made practically impossible. It was fortunate, in the circumstances, that the interruption of the scheduled landings on Yellow Beach had its counterpart in the delayed departure of the 1st BLT from its beachhead line. With coordinated action throughout the operation likely to be difficult, the battle awaiting the right elements of the 2d BLT might, in addition, bring them against the main enemy forces. It promised, in any case, to be a severe test for a first experience of combat.

Strong resistance was anticipated in the area behind Yellow Beach, for there the enemy had concentrated his principal installations (Map No. 9, inside back cover). Adjacent to On Chong's Wharf was the section assigned to the foe's construction troops, and near the sandspit and King's Wharf were the structures most used by the garrison. From the base of King's Wharf a secondary road crossed the island to the ocean shore. Between this road and the West Tank Barrier,

SECTION OF ANTITANK TRENCH, 6 ft. deep and over 14 ft. wide, forming part of two barrier defense systems at ends of "citadel" area on Butaritari. They ran part way across island and were extended by log fences (below). Our tanks crossed these barriers very easily.

1,100 to 1,200 yards further west, and between the lagoon and ocean shores, a distance of about 300 yards, the 2d BLT was expected on D Day to clear the enemy from whatever defenses he had established there. Advance estimate of the prepared defenses was necessarily inexact, for the tropical foliage concealed the precise locations and often even the existence of some of them. Only a few of the revetted underground shelters were spotted. The defenses just east of the West Tank Barrier clearing were incompletely forecast. But it was assumed that the enemy would be ready to oppose capture of that barrier with considerable strength.

In the area inland from the right half of Yellow Beach, and westward to the West Tank Barrier, advancing troops could expect to encounter four groups of buildings and storage dumps. The first group lay on the base of On Chong's Wharf and north of the highway, badly battered and burned by naval shelling. The second group consisted of ruined barracks and construction storehouses just south of the highway near the center of the beach. A third collection were placed on either side of a secondary road running southeast from On Chong's Wharf, and included barracks, mess hall, dispensary, and other service and administrative buildings for the labor force. The fourth and smallest group was that consisting of two barracks and a bath-house beside a curving trail nearer the West Tank Barrier clearing. Scattered among these structures, many of which were wrecked, were at least ten shelters as deeply excavated as the terrain permitted without water seepage across their floor; projecting only a foot or two above the ground, their upper parts were revetted sturdily in most cases with logs and earth.

The perimeter of this area contained the prepared firing positions; gun emplacements and rifle pits were along the lagoon shore between On Chong's Wharf and the tank trap clearing, in the West Tank Barrier system, and along the ocean shore. The beach between On Chong's Wharf and the clearing was covered by machine guns at the tip and on the base of On Chong's Wharf and by another at the lagoon end of the tank trap. On the ocean shore opposite the right half of Yellow Beach were three machine-gun emplacements and one antitank gun position, with adjacent rifle trenches. The estimates of the approximate strength of these defenses was nearly correct, although their sites were inexactly forecast, and more rifle trenches were expected than were actually found. The main position, however, was the West Tank Barrier system, the objective of the first day's operations.

The West Tank Barrier consisted of a deep, wide trench zigzagging through a clearing from the lagoon shore for three-fifths of the distance to the ocean, and of a heavy log barricade for the remainder of the distance. (See illustrations, p. 66.) The main highway crossed the trench at its northern end by an offset bridge, which was commanded by an antitank gun emplacement just south of the highway under the trees at the eastern edge of the clearing. (See illustration, p. 74.) Barbed wire was strung from low posts in the clearing along the eastern edge of the trench and under the trees just west of the clearing. Air observation had revealed most of this construction, and led to correct inference as to much of what lay concealed, such as the antitank emplacement at the northern end and the two machine guns at the southern end of the system, just east of the clearing. It was assumed that rifle trenches barred the eastern approach to the clearing, and one semicircular trench about 150 yards from it had been located. What was not known before the attack was the presence of a large underground shelter near this trench, nor the existence of some 50 rifle pits, interconnected by a bending trench running the full length of the clearing, just east of it. Knowledge of a pillbox in the center of this long trench, and of a machine-gun emplacement half way between it and the antitank emplacement at the northern end, was also lacking. The West Tank Barrier system turned out to be, on the whole, a stronger position than had been anticipated.

The disposition of enemy troops and the effectiveness of the air and naval bombardment remained to be discovered when the inland advance began. The pattern of resistance had not been revealed. Opposition to the western landings had been insignificant, all the way to the beachhead line. Was it concentrated in the area in front of the 1st BLT, or had it been reserved for the West Tank Barrier defenses? Had the air and naval bombardment left the capacity to defend that barrier basically unimpaired, or had the destruction wrought by bombs and shells discouraged a firm enemy stand there and caused him to retire farther east? Opposing fire at Yellow Beach had been harassing but not determined; the enemy had fallen back. But where? These questions were soon to be answered by the events of the battle for the West Tank Barrier.

From Yellow Beach to the West Tank Barrier

In the first few minutes of the landings the Alligators and the right wing detail of Special Detachment Z went rapidly toward the base of On Chong's Wharf. The riflemen then moved across an area from the beach to a point about half way across the island, pivoting on the base of the wharf and swinging to the right. Most of the squads met opposition only from snipers instead of the machine guns which they had been warned to expect. About 100 yards inland some of the attacking force encountered large, deep, revetted shelters (Map No. 9, inside back cover). They threw in grenades and, in addition to killing about 20 Korean laborers, took more than 30 prisoners among those who ran out. None of the shelters was entered, so that later in the day some enemy may have emerged to harass the rear. Two machine-gun positions and seven wholly or partly demolished buildings were found on the base of the wharf, all abandoned by the enemy.

As the special detachment was pivoting on the wharf, at its left Company F started to cross the island. The 1st and 2d Platoons, with two machine guns placed between them, and the 3d Platoon following in reserve support, moved almost due south. It took them until 1210 to reach the ocean after they had passed around the medium tanks, immobilized on the upper beach, and had begun their advance. They struggled through the debris and over the murky ground beyond the highway without coming to grips with the Japanese. The enemy remained out of sight, most of them withdrawing deeper into the woods, but a few snipers stayed in concealment among the tree tops.

The line of attack advanced from the right half of Yellow Beach with the 2d Platoon, Company F, on the left between Company E and the 1st Platoon, Company F. The rate of advance was uneven, for swifter movement was possible over the clear terrain under the tall coconut grove in the path of the 2d Platoon. Because the company could not use its damaged radios or keep in adequate contact through the service of messengers, a gap began to develop between the two platoons. The 3d Platoon was used to fill it instead of remaining in reserve. Elements of Company G and Company H were then used to support the movement. The 3d Platoon of Company G, reinforced by one light machine-gun squad, went at 1145 to the relief of the Special Detachment Z on the base of On Chong's Wharf, permitting that detail to retire to the beach area just east of the wharf. When shells from the *Dewey* began to land in its zone, the 3d Platoon was pulled back, but when the firing ceased, it returned to occupy the line from the lagoon inland for about 75 yards. The 1st Platoon, Company G, and men of the company's 60-mm mortar section and of Company H who took rifles and left their other weapons behind, moved to the center of the island and combed the area behind Company F for the snipers who remained there.

"Smoking out the snipers that were in the trees was the worst part of it," reported 1st Sgt. Pasquale J. Fusco. "We could not spot them even with glasses and it made our advance very slow. When we moved forward it was as a skirmish line, with each man being covered as he rushed from cover to cover. That meant that every man spent a large part of his time on the ground. While at prone, we carefully studied the trees and the ground. If one of our men began to fire rapidly into a tree or ground location, we knew that he had spotted a sniper, and those who could see the tree took up the fire. When we saw no enemy, we fired occasional shots into trees that looked likely."

Lt. Col. John F. McDonough left the battalion CP (see illustration, p. 70) in charge of subordinates and moved forward with the assault from the right half of Yellow Beach. When the ocean had been reached, the 2d Platoon, Company F, found no live installations but the 3d Platoon came upon two unoccupied, unused machine-gun emplacements, with a barbed wire barricade and a rifle trench, all abandoned by the enemy. Although these positions were primarily designed to resist a landing from the south and to control the use of the secondary road along the ocean shore, they could have been effectively used against the 3d Platoon. Between 1210 and 1230, Company F, reinforced, reorganized its southern movement into a line facing westward, prepared to close with the enemy in what promised to be the day's main battle. Farthest from Yellow Beach was the 1st Platoon, in the center, the 2d and 3d, and still on the extreme right, Special Detachment Z. The 3d Platoon, Company G, after acting with the other elements of that company in mopping up behind the front line, was brought forward between the 3d Platoon, Company F, and the Special Detachment Z. It straddled the highway.

The westward movement was strengthened by tank support. At noon Colonel McDonough left the line temporarily to talk directly to the tank crews at the beach. He summoned Capt. Wayne C. Sikes, a tank officer, to control their operations near the center of the line while Lt. Col. Harmon L. Edmondson, commanding the 193d Tank Battalion, led two mediums at once to the south shore. By 1230, five mediums had come to the ocean end of the line in response to a call from Capt. Francis P. Leonard of Company F. While crossing the island, they sprayed the trees with 37-mm fire, and upon coming up to the 1st Platoon, they sought the source of concealed heavy machine-gun and rifle fire, and also joined in cleaning out several shelters. An hour later Captain Sikes led other medium tanks against a strongly entrenched position in the center.

The Company F line had to advance between 300 and 400 yards to reach the tank-trap clearing. The first contact with its prepared

COMMAND POST MESSAGE CENTER *of 2d BLT in operation near Yellow Beach. Shelter consists of piles of ties and narrow-gauge iron rails salvaged by the enemy from an old railroad on Butaritari. The railroad had been used before the war in gathering copra for export.*

positions was at the southern end. There the 1st Platoon was aided by five medium tanks in quelling the heavy fire from advanced emplacements and rifle pits along the ocean shore. Once the tanks had suppressed this opposition, the infantry advanced swiftly and encircled the enemy's right flank by 1330. Japanese fire was far heavier in the center and at the northern end, where it fell most severely upon the 3d Platoon, Company F, and delayed the attainment of the clearing until late in the afternoon.

The semicircular trench and underground shelter in the center stopped the 3d Platoon almost as soon as it moved forward, and held it for two hours. Eight men were killed and six wounded as the attack opened. When Captain Sikes arrived, he courageously led the tanks forward on foot and in the face of enemy gun fire, and launched them in a confident, aggressive attack which continued for the remainder of the action. The infantry joined in assaulting the large shelter, deeply excavated in the higher ground at the center of the island. Hand grenades which they threw in were thrown back before exploding. The mechanism of a flame thrower failed. Direct shelling by 75-mm armor-piercing projectiles from a tank proved ineffective. Finally, a demolition squad of Company C, 102d Engineers, under 1st Lt. Thomas B. Palliser, arrived on the scene to try, for the first time in the whole operation, detonating a pole charge of TNT. Working together, one tank, two infantrymen with BAR's, and four engineers reduced the position by setting off the TNT in the entrance. The shelter was not collapsed but its 12 enemy occupants were killed.

A routine for knocking out fortified strongpoints was developed by one of the platoons of Company G. They found several consisting of "an open pit for a machine gun, a covered shelter, and a communication trench." The walls of the pits were from three feet to five feet in thickness and the trenches about four feet deep. The pits were usually connected with a very strong dugout revetted with sandbags and logs, and on the opposite end was another entrance somewhat below the surface of the earth.

"To knock out these emplacements, an eight-man squad would crawl to within about 15 yards of it and then take up station around it according to available cover. The BAR man and his assistant would cover the main entrance. Two men armed with grenades would make ready on both flanks of the shelter. They would rush the pit and heave grenades into it, then without stopping dash to the other side and blast the entrance with several more grenades. The other men did not fire unless essential. Once the grenades were exploded, the BAR man and assistant would follow up with bayonets. Two other men would inspect the pit with bayonets ready. The other four would lay back ready to fire. We did not lose a man in this type of action."

WELL-CONCEALED PILLBOXES *like this in West Tank Barrier defense system were overcome on D Day by coordinated action of engineers using TNT charges, and tanks and infantry furnishing covering fire. The way was thus cleared for the 1st and 2d BLT's to establish contact.*

As soon as the tanks and infantry in the center had taken the defensive area of the semicircular trench, they found themselves within a perimeter of persistent enemy fire coming from the central pillbox and its four flanking machine-gun nests, and from the rifle pits fringing the eastern edge of the barrier system. They were slowed down again.

The 3d Platoon, Company G, was at this stage sent into the line to advance with three medium tanks against the enemy's left wing. Underbrush was thick, and as they drew nearer the clearing, shell holes and debris increased. On each side of the highway machine-gun positions had been constructed. Two of them faced the lagoon between road and beach, and were connected by trench with a small shelter. They were quickly wiped out. The third had been built for an antitank gun, but as the troops advanced the barrel of a machine gun could be seen projecting from its concrete port.

ANTITANK GUN EMPLACEMENTS *were part of the barrier defense systems but were taken before being used against American tanks. Capture of one of these positions is described on page 75; its location in the West Tank Barrier is seen at (B) in illustration, page 78.*

Because of a misunderstanding the three tanks moved past this emplacement without attacking it; they drew no fire from the machine gun. S/Sgt. Michael Thompson, commanding the 3d Platoon, Company G, then crawled forward and rushed the emplacement. As he jumped in, he found himself in an open, 15-foot square, bounded by log walls 30 inches thick, except at 2 corners. In the corner nearest the road the thick concrete port from which the machine gun was extending interrupted the wall, while at the opposite corner was an opening leading into the barrier's protective trench system. Thompson grabbed the unmanned machine gun and swung it around to face the trench where some stupefied Japanese began to stir. Behind him a soldier who had been crawling also jumped in, only to shout: "I've been looking everywhere for one of these," snatch up a Japanese officer's saber from the floor, and disappear. Sgt. Thompson "never saw him again." The rest of the platoon came up as he moved down the trench, clearing it of Japanese.

The tanks which had left the emplacement undisturbed were able to continue across the barrier without serious opposition. At about 1600 they greeted in the clearing some light tanks which had come along the main highway from the western beaches. The enemy fire still covered the area and the tanks remained "buttoned up," but a preliminary junction of the two attacking forces was thus achieved. At the other end of the barrier, contact was made with Company B by 1500. In the center, a frontal attack by four medium tanks finally penetrated to the tank barrier trenchworks, and most of the enemy fire was silenced by 75-mm guns and 37-mm machine guns. All enemy resistance was crushed there by 1650. At 1755 the troops of the 1st and 2d BLT's had established contact all along the West Tank Barrier.

Advance to the West Tank Barrier from the West

At 1230, when the 2d BLT was in line facing the eastern edge of the West Tank Barrier, the 1st BLT was well along on its advance from the division beachhead line to the western edge of the tank-trap clearing. A series of positions advantageous for resistance to their advance had been reached without meeting the enemy. The ponds, marshes, and mangrove swamps which covered so much of the island in their zone narrowed the firm terrain at various points.

LIGHT TANKS *of Company C, 193d Tank Bn, are stalled for hours when moving to support the 1st Battalion Landing Team in its attack on the West Tank Barrier. The leading tank has become deeply mired in a shell hole in the main highway where it crosses one of the swamps.*

About 450 yards east of the division beachhead line at "Jill Lake" and again, some 700 yards farther east, at the second American phase line, the enemy could have set up positions easily covering the firm ground (Map No. 4, p. 13). The first of these opportunities had been taken; two machine-gun positions and an antitank-gun emplacement commanded the highway while fire trenches and another machine-gun nest covered the ocean shore and the area immediately to the north of it. But the enemy did not use these works to resist the advance of the 1st BLT, and had not even erected any fortified positions at the second phase line.

The American troops were opposed only by snipers. The 1st Platoon, Company C, 102d Engineers, accompanied the 1st BLT equipped with flame throwers and TNT pole charges for blasting out enemy pillboxes and shelters, but their services were not required. The sniper fire grew sharper as, about 1200, the 1st BLT reached the second phase line, with Company B on the right and Company C on the left. One man of Company C was killed, while Company B brought down two Japanese from their concealment in the tree tops.

For every sniper in the Makin operation who worked from a tree, there were ordinarily at least three others who fired from hiding behind bushes and logs. But in this particular area tree snipers were most prevalent. They had prepared among the fronds at the tops places where they sometimes cached rifles and left gourds of water and *saki*. To mark such trees, they tied girdles of fronds about four feet above the ground, so that a sniper could run to such a tree, snatch off the marker, climb up by notches cut in the trunk, and find everything awaiting him. The snipers were often barefoot, and several of them had painted their faces green. From the advancing Americans, they took a small toll in casualties.

The light tanks had not come forward with the 1st BLT beyond "Jill Lake," for in the highway between that pond and another, just north of it, a naval shell hole engulfed the leading tank of the column and acted as a thorough road block. (See illustration, p. 76.) The highway at that point was a causeway from which the other tanks could not depart to bypass the first one. It was necessary to extricate the semisubmerged vehicle and to fill up the shell hole before the column could proceed.

Patrols ahead of the second phase line failed to encounter any body of enemy troops, but the skirmish line was in contact with snipers at points all across the island, and Colonel Kelley, who had accompanied his advancing troops, was convinced that the Japanese would be met in force before the West Tank Barrier was reached.

To coordinate movement with the 2d BLT, observers on the lagoon shore kept watch on the progress of the Yellow Beach landings, reporting to Colonel Kelley, and he himself, with Lt. Col. James Roosevelt and Colonel Clark Ruffner, at about 1330 went to the shore to see at first hand. Seven landing barges were observed crossing the lagoon, and just after they had passed from view behind the hulks, heavy fire, probably from them, fell on the beach and grass around the three colonels, and cut short their observation.

At 1410 the tanks joined the ground troops, and as orders were received from Division Headquarters: "Continue your attack vigorously to effect a junction with McDonough without delay," the advance was resumed. Company B at the right of the line was about 200 yards nearer the West Tank Barrier clearing, nearly half a mile away. To the east could be heard the firing of Company F and its supporting tanks as they assailed the defenses from the rear.

Company B's attempt to approach the southern end of the clearing brought it, before long, within range of the fire from Company F. It sent forward patrols, being unable to establish contact with that company through any of the communications already in operation. For safety, it was obliged to take cover.

Company C made slower progress, for after some 500 yards it reached very difficult terrain, and when it came to a point about 250 yards from the barrier clearing, it ran upon stalwart enemy resistance. The Japanese had taken advantage of the cover offered by a zone of soft, swampy gullies, small pools, *bobai* patches, and some large trees to set up a machine gun in a well-concealed covert. The position was in a dip on slightly rising ground behind a *bobai* patch and a pool of water, while from trees around it, riflemen protected the machine-gun detail. The fire cut obliquely across the road, between two sharp

WEST TANK BARRIER *and approaches. Advancing with the 1st BLT, Col. J. G. Conroy, CO, 165th RCT, was killed in a clearing (A) by fire from a concealed MG (B). Strong defensive positions (C) delayed the 2d BLT, but the BLT's established flank contact (D) before 1500.*

bends, and stopped the 1st Platoon, Company C, in a small clearing north of the highway.

On the lagoon side of the road in the line of fire was a large palm tree which had around its base a square of heavy coconut logs and raised earth; 2d Lt. Daniel T. Nunnery took cover on the west side of this base and with his hand signalled to Colonel Kelley a warning to take cover, indicating the direction from which fire was coming.

Was this the beginning of an encounter with a substantial body of the enemy, which had fallen back from the western beaches and was now about to oppose American advance with vigor? Or was it merely another sniping position? Colonel Kelley believed that a considerable force was confronting Company C; Colonel Conroy came forward at this time and hastily concluded that only a single sniper was holding up the line. He was persuaded by Colonel Kelley that the opposition might be greater, and then decided to bring light tanks up to feel out the position, in spite of the danger that the tank fire might carry into the advanced right wing of the American line. While he withdrew to bring the tanks up, Colonel Kelley went to the boxed palm, and flung himself on the lagoon side of it as enemy fire quickened. Lieutenant Nunnery had been killed where he lay. Another man lay wounded in the open beyond him. From the shelter of a nearby tree, Chaplain Meany dashed across the road, hit the dirt beside the injured man, and started to give him assistance. Enemy bullets pierced the chaplain's arm and struck him in the chest, where a medal and an identification disc saved his life by deflecting them, but he fell limp. A soldier who tried to aid him was killed, and seven others were wounded at this juncture.

Four light tanks lumbered into the line of fire and passed a few feet beyond it before stopping. Then Colonel Conroy walked back into the scene, still upright, still believing that the Japanese fire was that of a lone sniper, and still shouting for the platoon to get forward. Just as Colonel Kelley had made his superior recognize the actual situation, and as Conroy seemed about to seek cover, he was struck between the eyes. By 1455 on D Day, the three BLT's of the 165th Infantry had lost their regimental commander.

For a moment Colonel Ruffner and Colonel Roosevelt tried to pull Colonel Conroy's body to safety, but Colonel Kelley shouted to them: "Let him go. He's dead!" Machine-gun and rifle fire was kicking up dirt on both sides of the boxed palm as Colonel Kelley and the other two colonels retired. Command of the regiment passed to Colonel Kelley, while that of the 1st BLT was assumed by its executive officer, Maj. James H. Mahoney. The tanks which Colonel Conroy had summoned also retired, without firing a shot, because of the likelihood of hitting friendly troops if they fired toward the supposed position of the enemy gun. Mortar fire, hand grenades, or even a machine-gun spraying of the area could not be used because American troops had infiltrated all around it.

Colonel Kelley ordered ten men of the regimental I and R Platoon under 1st Lt. Warren T. Lindquist to attack the position while other American troops withdrew. They were also to bring out Chaplain Meany. Locating the Lewis gun in a shallow depression ringed with brush, they flung two grenades against it but could not observe the effects. They then started to move upon a supporting enemy gun but retired when a Company C machine gun began to fire into the area. Instead, they found Father Meany and brought him safely to a waiting vehicle where medics gave him plasma. It was too dark for evacuation by that time, so the I and R Platoon furnished a protective perimeter for the night about 300 yards west of the boxed palm.

While the 1st Platoon, Company C, was held up, the 2d and 3d Platoons advanced to the edge of the West Tank Barrier clearing. Enemy resistance was weakening there, and the two platoons were able to move along the clearing and surround such forces as might have remained in the area uncovered by the 1st Platoon.

Company A, which had been in reserve throughout the first phase of the attack, advanced at 1500 from its position near "Rita Lake" and acted as a mopping-up force in the rear of Company B. By the time it had come up to Company B, at the ocean end of the clearing, that unit had established contact with the 1st Platoon, Company F, on the opposite side of the barrier. At about 1700, after the enemy in the center were destroyed, contact between the BLT's extended the length of the barrier.

The first portion of the plan for occupying Butaritari Island was accomplished, therefore, late on D Day. In the entire zone from the western beaches to the center of the "citadel" area, enemy resistance had been overcome except for one small wedge-shaped pocket northwest of the West Tank Barrier clearing. On orders from Division Headquarters hostilities were broken off and positions for the night were selected and secured.

Holding Action to the East

Upon landing at Yellow Beach, the 2d BLT had divided into two forces of which one, as has been described, moved right toward a junction with the 1st BLT after assault upon the West Tank Barrier. The second moved to the left to take up a holding position. This left-wing force consisted of Company E, 165th Infantry, half of the Special Detachment Z, 105th Infantry, and, before the end of the day, a platoon of light tanks. On the beach, in reserve, elements of Heavy Weapons Company H were available.

The mission of the 1st Platoon, Company E, was to push directly across the atoll to the ocean shore, while maintaining contact with Company F on its right (Map No. 9a, inside back cover). It was then to turn left and to act as company reserve behind the 2d Platoon. The 2d Platoon was expected to move inland 50 yards beyond the highway, and at that point to swing left and to extend its line to the ocean shore, forming the right platoon of the force by which the eastern half of the island would be sealed off from the remainder. One reinforced squad from the 3d Platoon was to mop up the sand-spit and the remainder to advance left, occupying a position in the line between the 2d Platoon on its right and Detachment Z on its left. By nightfall Company E was expected to reach a line along a dirt road crossing the island from King's Wharf, an advance of about 500 yards east of Yellow Beach. With Colonel McDonough directing the drive on the West Tank Barrier, and Major Claire, designated to command Company E, detained in the lagoon while the hulks were under fire, actual command during most of D Day fell to Capt. Bernard Ryan, company commander.

The 1st Platoon's zone contained no buildings within the first 120 yards of advance, and only two fortified positions near the main island highway on its left flank. These were soon found to be out of action: one of them, for a machine gun, had been rendered inoperative by the bombardment, or had been abandoned, while the other, containing a 37-mm gun, was an antitank position commanding the main island highway. The gun was mounted on wheels, and had been disabled; its cover was still on. It had not been manned. The men advanced some 12 to 14 yards every 5 minutes, under scattered coconut trees and through light underbrush, from which they were subject to sniping fire. About halfway across the island they came

ACTION FROM EASTERN HALF OF YELLOW BEACH *on D Day* *brought three platoons of Co E, 165th Infantry, on a line across the island. In the area shown the 3d Platoon met stiff resistance at a "tunnel-like emplacement" from which the enemy were finally driven.*

AREA 'X'

upon a group of *bobai* pits, and beyond them, a thick grove of coconut palms extending through to the ocean. Near the ocean shore road storage buildings for bombs and food were found undefended, but the enemy was occupying a defensive position beyond the road at the very end of the platoon's route across the island. There a machine-gun emplacement which was designed principally to rake the ocean approach, and which was flanked by rifle pits and by double-apron barbed wire, was turned against the Americans approaching from the north.

The platoon had sustained three killed and one wounded from snipers as they crossed the island, the enemy timing his fire so that the sound would be masked by airplane passes and the din of other American operations. In the machine-gun emplacement and the associated rifle pits, ten Japanese were killed. A medium tank fired its 75-mm gun into the entrance to silence the emplacement.

The 2d Platoon met even lighter opposition in an area having less enemy installations, and moved slowly forward to take up the position planned for it on the right of the cross-island line. Three men were wounded in this phase. At the end, the platoon was held up until the 3d Platoon could fill in the gap at its left.

Mopping up the sandspit area ("Area X") proved to be an easy task for the reinforced squad from the 3d Platoon, Company E. All resistance there had been destroyed previously by the air and naval bombardment and by the Alligator detail. The mopping-up unit worked carefully among the wreckage of the large barracks, a building for the enemy commander and his staff, two wireless installations, small storehouses, and a telephone exchange. A machine-gun emplacement on the roof of a bomb shelter, near the corner of the sandspit and the cove beach, had been knocked out. The larger radio station was without a roof and in disorder. Its mission readily completed, the "Area X" detail waited for the left wing of the Company E line to move along the beach as far as the base of the sandspit.

Eventually, when the company had established contact with Special Detachment Z at the base of King's Wharf, the 3d Platoon detail expected to leave the sandspit and join in the eastward advance. The line never got that far, however, and the special detachment, like the "Area X" detail, remained isolated for several hours. At 1430 the right element of the special detachment came from On Chong's

Wharf to join the left element, and both portions withdrew from the base of King's Wharf shortly afterward when they were pulled back to avoid being hit by a forthcoming artillery barrage. The 3d Platoon detail, in a less exposed position on the sandspit, waited out the barrage. One badly aimed shell landed among them, killing three men and wounding three or four.

The artillery had been called upon to lay a barrage in the area just west of the King's Wharf road. There, the main portion of the 3d Platoon, Company E, was stopped. It ran upon the day's most difficult ground fighting at a position strongly constructed and cleverly disguised, lying directly opposite the sandspit, south of the main island highway. (See illustration, p. 82.) Near the road was a revetment for one of the two Japanese tankettes on the island, with five rifle pits beside it. A few yards east was the position which gave the most trouble. At a bend in the highway was a machine gun, facing west, which delivered enfilading fire upon the 3d Platoon. Adjoining the emplacement, to the south, was a large *bobai* pit. The earth from the pit seemed to have been piled up along its western edge in a curving mound about 8 feet high, extending, as the men discovered, about 35 yards from the machine-gun position to a concrete pillbox nearer the center of the island (Map No. 9, inside back cover).

While most of the platoon remained pinned down, several men approached the mound from the extreme right of the *bobai* pit without drawing fire. They discovered a kneeling trench about 2 feet deep and 15 feet long, cut diagonally across the top of the mound, in which 3 men took cover temporarily. Beneath them, and unknown to them, ran a tunnel connecting the machine gun with the pillbox position. The convex eastern side of the mound contained a series of apertures which they had not yet seen, commanding a clearing farther east, and along the top were still others just large enough for a man to squeeze through. Before these apertures were noticed, several Japanese suddenly emerged while the three Americans were trying to locate the machine-gun fire, and charged with bayonets. Before they had been cut down by fire from the platoon, they had killed one and wounded another. Machine-gun fire then protected a second set of enemy as they bayoneted to death the wounded man and slashed the third man on the mound. The rest of the infiltrating party withdrew.

Bazookas and rifle grenades were tried against the emplacement with no effect. Its triple-thick walls of coconut logs, covered with earth, were impervious. Since the entire line was being held up, artillery fire from the Ukiangong Point position, and mortar fire from Yellow Beach, were requested to deny the enemy any opportunity to gather reinforcements and to counterattack. Communications operated promptly and effectively. The enemy were cut off from the east by a barrage from the 105th Field Artillery.

Sgt. Hoyl Mersereau next led a detail of six or seven men past the long tunnel to the shelter of a low bank about 40 yards east. By creeping and crawling they reached a position from which they could fire into the tunnel openings from the east. Flame throwers were unavailable because, after other difficulties had been overcome, their oxygen tanks were all misplaced on the beach. But the combat engineers exploded TNT blocks in the machine-gun nests

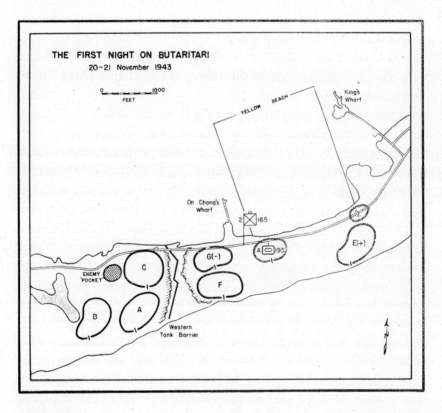

MAP NO. 6

at either end, and light tanks fired 37-mm shells into the entrances until the enemy began making desperate sorties, charging with bayonets upon soldiers who cut them down with rifle fire. At 1600, some four hours after the tunnel was first encountered, it was possible to leave it covered by a detail while the rest of the 3d Platoon moved forward. Eight casualties had been sustained.

. One hundred and fifty yards farther east was an underground CP and bomb shelter, with telephone, radio, and electric lights. The platoon advanced and took it quickly, but before they could reach the road, the line of advance marked out for D Day, they came under fire which stopped them. Directly in front of them, the thickness of the woods made the terrain seem undesirable for an all-night position. Under orders at 1720 to cease action and to take secure positions until next day, Company E withdrew to an area south of the sandspit's western edge, and near the center of the island. As it was digging in for the night, a platoon of Company G appeared to reinforce it.

Company E had contained the enemy in the eastern part of the main defensive area, even though its line of advance fell short of the road from King's Wharf to the ocean. Four of the medium tanks did penetrate almost to that position. They had worked with Company F until the ocean end of the West Tank Barrier was subdued, and had then gone east along the shore road, blazing at likely targets on the ground and in the trees; being unaccompanied by infantry, they turned back and went to spend the night with a tank park near Yellow Beach. Infantry and tanks together were to resume the advance next day.

Situation at the Close of D Day

As the night closed the first day's operations on Butaritari Island, the infantry elements established defensive perimeters and settled down to wait for dawn. Since early afternoon, the 3d BLT had been assembled in divisional reserve southwest of "Rita Lake." General Ralph C. Smith had ordered it to be prepared to move from Yellow Beach to Kuma Island at 0900 next morning, but General Holland M. Smith, with Admiral Turner's concurrence, disapproved the project, stating that it was necessary to retain one battalion in readiness to aid the operation at Tarawa.

Of the 1st BLT, Companies A, B, and D bivouacked in adjacent areas on the ocean side of the island, west of the West Tank Barrier. Company C, however, set up its position in the northern half of the barrier clearing, just east of the "pocket" of still active Japanese (Map No. 6, p. 86).

Just east of the barrier's northern extremity, Company G developed its perimeter, after one of its platoons had gone to the support of Company E. Directly south of Company G in the same area was Company F. At least 1,000 yards farther east was the position established by Company E and one platoon of Company G. North of them, maintaining a line from the highway to the lagoon, were the consolidated details of Special Detachment Z of the 105th Infantry.

The 105th Field Artillery dug in for the night near their guns, south of Ukiangong village. Not far from them was the Alligator CP of the 193d Tank Battalion. The tanks and Alligators were gathered together near each of the main beaches. The reserve platoon of light tanks at Red Beach 2 had been out of contact with the others since 1330, and was expecting action early next day. The mediums reassembled, after their separate forays of the day, inland from Yellow Beach and not far from the CP of Colonel McDonough.

FOX HOLES ON YELLOW BEACH *are dug by members of shore party as they prepare for their first night. Note signal markers in background. (Below) Along the highway behind beach, tanks, bulldozers, and jeeps are parked wherever shell holes and debris do not prevent.*

General Ralph C. Smith came ashore at 1830 and moved up to the forward echelons. The communications problems still existing made it advisable to delay the moving of Division Headquarters from the *Leonard Wood* until next day.

Supply conditions at the beaches were disturbing. Although on the average the transports were one-fourth unloaded, many of the barges, LST's, and LCT's, to which cargo had been shifted, remained to be unloaded later because they could not get to the beaches or use any of the wharves. Early in the afternoon, operations on Red Beach 1 had become merely the salvaging of what had foundered earlier on the reef. Nothing could be landed on Red Beach 2 after 1700, and many barges had sat off shore for hours waiting in vain for their turn to unload into LVT's and thus have their cargoes taken over the impassable reef. Loaded barges, LST's, and the *Alcyone* were ordered into the lagoon for the night, where they lay at anchor and continued to wait.

Quartermaster and Ordnance dumps had been set up on Red Beach 2, but the ammunition for the 105-mm guns of the 105th Field Artillery needed hauling to the position on Ukiangong Point. Gasoline for the LVT's would be needed next day. Too few trucks and bulldozers had come ashore to accomplish all the pressing tasks requiring them. The clearing station team was ashore, but its equipment remained on the transport, packed in two trucks.

Yellow Beach had not been far developed, for what it lacked in roughness was counterbalanced by the facts that it had been repeatedly under fire, that its 300 yards of width led quickly to an inland area of no great depth, across which troops were moving, and lastly, that its reef made necessary a long drag ashore by LVT's, at least until King's Wharf could be converted to use by the invaders.

At 1705 air patrols ceased. The transports and warships moved out to sea, maintaining patrols against enemy submarines and air attacks. Radio silence was resumed. The landing forces were "on their own" until morning.

Using artillery, tanks, the command of the air, and overwhelming numbers, the invaders had driven the enemy before them. The use of force had been economical and casualties were relatively light (25 killed and 62 wounded seriously enough to be taken out of action), but the troops were tired. They had been roused before dawn, had made their first landing on a hostile beach under fire, and had moved through the island's marshes and tropical growth during hours of incessant strain. Many of them had abandoned heavy packs, rations and all, and had gone without food all day. Some were "trigger-happy," and none knew just what to expect of the enemy now that darkness would cloak his movements; on every side the advent of night was greeted by increasing small-arms fire.

The men dug in for the night expecting the next day's fighting to be more severe. Not all of them were thorough in the digging. One of them, as he later told the chaplain, thought that the Lord would not approve of his job. "God, if you only let me live until tomorrow," he prayed, "I'll guarantee that this damned fox hole will be deeper by morning."

Some of the enemy remained in the area between the tank barriers even after it had been passed over by the initial line of assault and by one or more mopping-up details. They may have continued to hide in the tree tops, for snipers there tended to withhold their fire until it could be delivered on scattered skirmishers, or, as happened

BATTALION MEDICAL AID STATION *near Yellow Beach in an old bobai pit, lined with grass and palm fronds. Wounded were taken from aid station to transport until noon of 2d day, when a clearing station and surgical service had been installed on Ukiangong Point to treat them.*

in one instance, on the surgeon at work in the aid station established near Yellow Beach. Some certainly lurked in the shelters among the dead. Late that afternoon, when two officers were sitting on a dugout swapping experiences, one of them jumped to his feet. "There's something under here," he said, and just then a machine gun opened up upon some of the beach party who were still bringing supplies inshore. He slipped around to the rear of the mound and found an opening covered by a curtain. Lifting the curtain with his left hand, he threw a grenade inside with his right. Almost at the same instant, just before the grenade exploded, one of the enemy fired a pistol shot which grazed the lieutenant's arm.

Mopping-up activities in the "citadel" area were incomplete as the first night arrived. The enemy was believed capable of defending his present positions to the death, withdrawing to the east on Butaritari and crossing to Kuma Island, or even of counterattack.

Enemy opposition on D Day revealed both weakness and disorganization. During the first air strike, antiaircraft artillery troops suspended firing, abandoned their guns, fled to the eastern OP, and took refuge in its air raid shelter. Many of the enemy, especially the Korean labor troops, cowered in shelters even after the bombardment had ceased. The landings on Yellow Beach received relatively strong resistance, but even there withdrawal was unavoidable soon after the touchdown. The enemy then left snipers in scattered positions and gathered the main portion of his forces opposite the left wing of the invading troops. A smaller detachment was left in the West Tank Barrier to resist the junction of the 1st and 2d BLT's; the air and naval bombardment had greatly weakened the detachment by causing heavy casualties among those in open emplacements and trenches. Thus on D Day the firmest enemy opposition was that encountered by the smallest of the attacking elements, Company E.

The Drive Eastward

The First Night

THE FIRST NIGHT ON BUTARITARI was marked by energetic enemy activity. No air attacks were delivered, the limited air power of the Japanese having been concentrated on the Southern Carrier Force off Tarawa, but ground fighting was continuous. Some of the enemy who had been left during the day's fighting in the western area tried to work their way eastward to rejoin their own forces. Others moved back from the east into areas which had been cleared on D Day, either to harass the invaders in their many fox holes or to set up machine guns in positions of advantage for the following morning. Before the night was over, they had succeeded in preparing at least seven such positions, and had infiltrated into the company perimeters enough to inflict a few casualties and cause much sleepless anxiety.

Moving in total darkness, the Japanese used many ruses to discover the hidden locations of the American troops. The men had been ordered to observe complete silence. They even struggled to control their coughs by chewing on handkerchiefs and shirtsleeves. When an armed Japanese came to a perimeter and called out, as several did: "Psst! Hey, Sarge!" he was therefore readily recognized as an impostor and shot. Although this disposed of that offender, the spurts of flame from rifles revealed targets at which other Japanese promptly fired rifles or threw grenades. At some points snipers in trees dropped firecrackers, the explosions of which resembled Japanese rifle fire enough to draw response from excited Americans. Snipers then shot into the fox holes revealed by gun flashes. When one captive was taken to the 1st Battalion aid station, he attracted enemy fire by making loud animal noises until he was clubbed into silence.

"Medics! Medics! Send a medic out here," some of them called; and others, "Hey, Charlie! Where's my buddy?" As daylight

ENEMY DUAL-PURPOSE GUN *on base of King's Wharf, and behind it, in cove, wreck of a Japanese seaplane in which snipers gathered during the first night of the operation. Their fire on the 2d BLT was stopped finally by an explosion caused by shells fired from our tanks.*

approached, their boldness increased. One crawled to the edge of a fox hole and, as he was observed, blurted out: "Me no got gun." He was instantly shot, and fortunately so, as morning showed that he had died while taking aim. Another foolhardy enemy soldier, just before dawn, used irresistibly fighting language by walking along the lagoon shore shouting: "Reveille, fellows! Get up! Reveille!"

Some patrols were intercepted. One of from 12 to 16 men was stopped when it tried to work around Company E's left flank, near the sandspit. Others tried vainly to infiltrate nearer the lagoon through the road-to-shore line of Detachment Z, 105th Infantry. A 12-man patrol slipped along the ocean shore or came south from the "pocket" to a point between Companies A and B. Only 20 feet from Company A, it sniped all night at Company B in its front, and when detected in prone positions at dawn, all its members were surprised and killed. In the rear of Company B's area, another patrol of ten was discovered at 0700, advancing through the woods in single file. Two men destroyed it with a BAR and some hand grenades.

In the Yellow Beach area, snipers killed two tank men, who had left a fox hole to pursue an enemy soldier infiltrating into the tank park, and a third, as he climbed out of a tank shortly before dawn and became visible in the pale light of a waning moon.

Much aimless shooting by "trigger-happy" men also occurred in that part of the island. In the early morning its volume increased. Just after daylight, a man from the 152d Engineers ran along the lagoon shore from the direction of On Chong's Wharf toward the 2d BLT CP, shouting: "There's a hundred and fifty Japs in the trees." A wave of shooting hysteria swept the area, and men started firing at bushes and trees until the place was "simply ablaze with fire." When the engineer admitted that he had seen no enemy but merely "had heard firing," shouted orders to the men to cease firing proved ineffectual. Direct commands to each individual soldier were necessary. The harassing tactics of the enemy had been effective.

The enemy was also successful in mounting machine guns in damaging positions. Two were set up near the lagoon, between the West Tank Barrier and the first bend of the road to the west of it. Five other machine-gun positions were established in the area around the sandspit and King's Wharf. The wreck of a Japanese four-motored "Emily" (see illustration, p. 94) in the sandspit cove was utilized, as were a building on the sandspit, another building near the base of King's Wharf, and two emplacements at the base of the wharf and near the hospital structure there.

Preparing the Second Day's Attack

Before sunrise, the *Yorktown's* dawn patrol was in the air. In less than half an hour it had shot down a large Japanese reconnaissance plane a few miles from Makin. Vessels of the Task Force reappeared. Barges began coming to the beaches, and those which approached Yellow Beach "returned" fire upon the two hulks as they passed. On Kuma Island, near which they had spent the night in a small craft, Maj. Jacob H. Herzog and a reconnaissance detail landed

and commenced their investigation.[1] Near Red Beach 2 Col. Charles
B. Ferris, divisional G–4, assembled the special staff at 0600 and
established the day's program for meeting supply problems, policing
the roads, and caring for enemy dead. In the Yellow Beach area
these were estimated at 200, while the main Japanese force was
thought to be in positions within the "citadel" area just west of the
East Tank Barrier.

---

[1] Air reconnaissance on D Day reported no military installations on Little Makin or
any other island in Makin except Butaritari.

MEDIUM TANKS SHELLING KING'S WHARF *as the second day's operations commence at Makin. During the night Japanese machine gunners had infiltrated to positions at end of wharf from which, at dawn, they began firing on landing barges. The 75-mm shells silenced them.*

The problem of supply for the second day's action was difficult. The highway from the western shore had been under repair and was available for quarter-ton traffic by 0904. It was, however, under interdictory fire from Japanese snipers in the unreduced "pocket" (Map No. 6, p. 86), and perhaps from others. Had the approach to Yellow Beach been secure, the high water of morning might have been advantageously used; extraordinary efforts by the shore party might have built up the dumps to meet the requirements of the two BLT's operating in that area. But landing on Yellow Beach remained distinctly hazardous.

The two hulks on the reef near On Chong's Wharf, which had been so heavily attacked from the air and the sea on D Day, were believed once more to have been made an active enemy firing position. As barges came in to Yellow Beach early on the second morning, some of them "returned" fire upon the hulks, aiming at their top decks. On shore, among troops stationed in and near the West Tank Barrier clearing during the night, intermittent bursts of machine-gun fire were received for as much as two hours after dawn. They may have been "overs" directed toward the hulks from the barges. At 0818, while the barges stayed clear, the first of a long series of air strikes which continued until 1630 that afternoon began against the hulks. At 0920 some of the medium tanks went to the water's edge and shelled the hulks with their "75's." They were reported to be overshooting by some 2,000 yards, furnishing a fire which boats entering the lagoon were unexpectedly obliged to face. Whether from enemy or friendly fire, the approach to Yellow Beach was so dangerous for the small barges that, as late as 1230, about 40 of them were circling well out in the lagoon waiting for the signal to come in, and by that time the tide was ebbing.

To free the line to Red Beach 2, an effort to destroy the Japanese in the "pocket" began as soon as heavy fire believed to be from the enemy there opened at 0800, upon Company C. S/Sgt. Emanuel F. De Fabees and a patrol went into the pocket from the east, and then again, from the northeast, in each instance finding fire too severe to continue. In some manner not recorded, it became possible for Major Mahoney, 1st BLT commander, to report at 0840 that Company C had terminated opposition from the "pocket" and was taking steps to contain the area while it was combed for hiding snipers.

The boldest sniper action came from a coconut grove along the eastern edge of the West Tank Barrier clearing, just north of the middle of the island. At about 1030 a group of Japanese opened up with rifles and light machine guns upon the 1st Platoon, Company F, inflicting no casualties but promoting determined steps to silence them. Stray shots came flying into Company F's CP near the center of the island, and Captain Leonard therefore asked urgently for three light tanks to move against the source. To reach a position from which they could fire canister into the grove without endangering friendly troops, the tanks moved to the northern end of the clearing, beside the highway; their line of fire was then toward the ocean.

About five minutes after they began spraying the tree tops, under directions from 1st Lt. Edward J. Gallagher as he stood on one of the tanks, a fourth tank came along the highway with fuel in tow. Its cable snapped. Capt. Charles B. Tobin and Sgt. John S. Sloane climbed out of it to investigate and at once came under sniper fire. The three other tanks covered them while they crawled back into their own vehicle.

Before the four tanks had dispersed, a navy bomber suddenly swung over them at a very low altitude, and from its opening bomb-bay hatch, a 2,000-lb. "daisy-cutter" fell, striking ground about 25 feet from Captain Tobin's tank on the highway. Lieutenant Gallagher, Pfc. John E. Costello, who was covering him from the base of a nearby tree, and Cpl. Elmer F. Conway, who was in a fox hole, were all killed, and two sergeants were wounded, while other tank men were injured by the concussion. By the time the crews had recovered the snipers were forgotten. They gave no further trouble.

The plan of attack for the second day provided that Company E and attached elements should push along the island toward the East Tank Barrier, while Company F remained in reserve near Yellow Beach; the 1st BLT was to clean out the snipers near the West Tank Barrier and thence westward toward the Red Beaches. Hopes of an early start were disappointed, for Colonel McDonough elected to defer the advance of the infantry until the tanks were ready, and these were delayed until enough fuel could be brought to them for the projected advance. The artillery barrage which began at 0700 was continued until 0820, and resumed from 0945 until 1010, with 783 rounds fired by nine 105-mm howitzers.

At 0835 bombing and strafing of the area ahead of Company E as far as the East Tank Barrier were requested at once. They were quickly supplied, and only when the tank fuel had arrived at 1000 and the tanks were almost ready was the time of the attack advanced from 1100 to 1045. Stoppage of air support was requested at 1023; "Tanks and troops moving forward" was given as the reason. Although this request was acknowledged and confirmed, the air column formed for the bombing runs over the area kept coming as originally ordered.

Enemy machine-gun positions came under preparatory attack from both tanks and planes. At 0902 some of the medium tanks fired from the water's edge upon the building near the end of King's Wharf (see illustration, p. 96), in which a gun had been put up during the night. At the same time, planes were strafing the corresponding positions on Stone Pier, which they attacked repeatedly from 0910 to 1100.

By 1110 the attack was in progress. Ten medium tanks had been refueled and moved to position in support of the troops. The troops had emerged from their slit trenches as the planes roared off and the dropping of 2,000-lb. "daisy-cutters" came to an end.

The Second Day's Advance

At 1100 the marines and the reinforced 2d Platoon, Company G, who had returned from Tukerere Island to the *Neville* for the night, reported to Colonel McDonough and were sent into the attack. The 1st BLT was then waiting for the last of the air bombing. The line

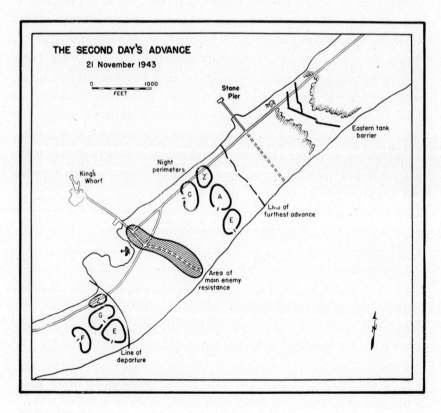

THE SECOND DAY'S ADVANCE
21 November 1943

MAP NO. 7

soon formed and advanced eastward with the medium tanks at either flank (Map No. 7, p. 100). On the extreme left was Special Detachment Z, 105th Infantry. Next to it came the 1st Platoon, Company G, which had reinforced the 3d Platoon, Company E, throughout the night. In the right center was the 1st Platoon, and on the right wing, the 2d Platoon, both of Company E. All units moved forward in skirmish line. Fifty yards back, mopping up the Japanese snipers, was a second formation consisting of the 3d Platoon, Company E, and the 2d and 3d Platoons of Company G, and the marines. They moved first over the area covered late on the previous afternoon, from which Company E had withdrawn for its secure night position.

The line advanced steadily and aggressively, but slowly, averaging about three yards a minute. "On the second day we did not allow sniper fire to deter us," explained 1st Sgt. Thomas E. Valentine of the front echelon of Company E. "We had already found that the snipers were used more as a nuisance than an obstacle. They would fire, but we noted little effect by way of casualties. We learned that by taking careful cover and moving rapidly from one concealment to another we could minimize the sniper threat. Moreover, we knew that our reserves would get them if we did not. So we contented ourselves with firing at a tree when we thought a shot had come from it and we continued to move on. Our reserves could check on whether we had killed him or not."

In the area west of the underground CP, which had been covered during the previous afternoon and then relinquished for the night, the enemy once more fell back. In the next 200 yards, however, from the CP to the road which crossed the island from the base of King's Wharf, the stiffest resistance of the day was met. In spite of the artillery and air bombardment, the enemy delivered a strong fire in this area from several positions, including those prepared during the night.

From the battered Japanese seaplane which was beached in the cove at the left, flanking machine-gun and rifle fire struck at the left wing and carried in toward the center (see illustration, p. 94). Other efforts failing, four of the medium tanks pumped enough shells from their "75's" at close range to annihilate the 18 occupants.[1] On the right, in an emplacement intended mainly for defense against

---

[1] From the air an explosion in the seaplane was observed at 1146.

OBSERVATION TOWER *at the base of King's Wharf from which enemy snipers were cleared quickly during the advance on D plus 1:*

landings from the ocean, three dual-purpose, 3-inch guns were operated from the ocean shore for a while, but were eventually abandoned
amid a litter of empty shells before the infantry closed in. Beyond
these guns, at the ocean end of the cross-island road, a twin-barreled,
13-mm, dual-purpose machine gun also covered part of this zone of
advance.

In the center about 30 yards beyond the CP was a large underground shelter, and about 30 yards farther, 6 rifle pits connected by a trench. Squarely across the King's Wharf road, a little south of the middle of the island and running east and west, was a longer trench with 11 rifle pits. At the left center, as they approached the road, the 3d Platoon, Company G, entered a grove of hardwood trees which stretched on toward the East Tank Barrier, while in the right center and on to the ocean, the 1st and 2d Platoons, Company E, moved among coconuts and small clearings. There, as well as in the prepared emplacements, Japanese machine gunners took temporary positions, and snipers fired persistently.

Detachment Z, 105th Infantry, on the extreme left, was ordered to move along the lagoon shore in the area where Japanese had infiltrated during the preceding night. Its responsibilities included

MANY BOMB SHELTERS *were constructed like this on Butaritari. Larger dugouts were used as machine-gun emplacements. During air strikes on 19 November the enemy entered many and remained until blasted out by grenades, TNT pole charges, or shells from our tanks.*

JAPANESE RADIO TRANSMITTING STATION *for long-range communication was situated in this heavily revetted frame structure near center of Butaritari Island. It was the counterpart of a long-range receiving station located within main fortified area near King's Wharf.*

the base of King's Wharf, on which three dual-purpose guns and one antiaircraft gun were placed, and on which three machine guns had also been installed during the night.

The operations of the advancing front consisted principally of eliminating pillboxes, dugouts (see illustration, p. 103), and log-revetted emplacements. Coordination between tanks and infantry ran much more smoothly than on the previous day. The infantry made frequent use of the offensive grenade, which raised a covering dust even when it fell short of the intended target. Thus hidden, men moved to the flanks and rear of the pillboxes. BAR fire, machine-gun fire, and that from the tanks covered details crawling forward with blocks of TNT. When these charges were exploded at the entrances of installations, they either killed the occupants or sealed the exits. Occasionally the tanks rode onto the shelters to crush them with sheer weight. The tanks were used at all needed points along the line from ocean to lagoon.

Ahead of the advance, the artillery on Ukiangong Point sent a creeping barrage from the King's Wharf road to the East Tank Barrier. Although no direct hits of significance fell upon pillboxes and shelters, the enemy was kept under cover. Japanese artillery was noticeably lacking, and enemy mortar fire was infrequent.

Between noon and 1400, the advance passed through the area containing the structures of greatest importance to the Japanese. On the bulge in the lagoon shore from which ran the base of King's Wharf, along the island highway to the east, and in an angle formed by the highway and the King's Wharf road were the buildings used by the Japanese aviation personnel, and stores of fuel and ammunition. A set of hospital buildings was situated near the lagoon at the base of the wharf. Under coconut trees along the ocean shore at the right were two machine-gun emplacements, supported by ten rifle pits, the whole group being protected on the east and west flanks by double-apron wire running inland from the water across the ocean shore road. One after another, all the positions were overrun.

692414°—46—8

INTERIOR OF ENEMY RADIO STATION *shown on opposite page, with six complete transmitters arranged along the outside walls, from which antenna leads could be short. Cables were in trenches in the concrete floor; power distribution panel was on inside wall of this room.*

The enemy fought ineffectively as Company E and attached elements pushed steadily and thoroughly ahead. In its rear, Company A relieved Company F as battalion reserve at 1300, and moved to a mopping-up position some 200 yards west of the front line without incident. The worst of the enemy resistance had been met and overcome by 1400. Near the aviation CP, Detachment Z found at that time a circle of six dead Japanese officers, probably air pilots, who had killed themselves, or each other, with revolvers. Working with the tanks, the line moved on for three more hours until it was about 1,000 yards from Yellow Beach and 200 yards short of Stone Pier and its cross-island road. By 1730, a halt was called. It was again time to prepare defenses for the night.

The day's success wrested from the Japanese their largest radio receiving installation, a heavily revetted underground building, 78 feet by 33 feet, which lay at the northwestern corner of a 200-foot clearing east of the King's Wharf road, near two 60-foot masts (Map No. 9). With nine receivers of identical type, it was the counterpart of a new transmitting station beyond the East Tank Barrier.

Other installations captured or destroyed left the main area of enemy military positions entirely in American possession. Before them now was the East Tank Barrier system, resembling that at the west, but designed primarily to stop an assault from the east. Once it had been taken from the rear, little would remain except the radio transmitter station and the outpost defenses, scattered over the remaining half of the island. The buildings along the lagoon near the Government Wharf were old British structures erected for civilian purposes. Tanimaiaki village also lay ahead near the eastern tip (Map No. 8, p. 110). At a cost of 26 wounded and 18 killed in battle, not including those killed and wounded by bombing accidents,[1] the second day's advance had consumed enough of the enemy's waning power to make certain that the third day's operations would be conclusive.[2] No withdrawal to the east on any sizable scale had been observed from the air during the day; presumably the enemy were to stand in the East Tank Barrier system.

---

[1] The medical report for 21 November shows that of the 15 received at the clearing station, 2 died and 13 were wounded.

[2] No estimate of enemy casualties was officially computed, but isolated reports of those killed by the bombardment, by American ground fighting, and by their own suicidal hands total 54.

The Second Night

The second night on Butaritari approached with the problem of supply still unsolved, but with Yellow Beach at last free of fire from the much battered hulks. They were reconnoitered late in the afternoon by a patrol of 16 men from Company C under 2d Lt. Everett W. McGinley. The patrol went out in two Alligators, boarded the structures, and discovered the top deck of each to be so wrecked and twisted that "no enemy could have fired from it without being in plain view." No evidence of enemy occupation was found, and the patrol returned with a negative report.[1] The fire which had been attributed to enemy emplaced there was quieted by nightfall.

On Red Beach 2, a bulldozer worked late under artificial light to clear the beach for the next day. After first ordering the transfer of unloading operations from all vessels except the *Pierce* from Red Beach 2 to Yellow Beach, Admiral Turner was persuaded to revise the plan and permit the fullest use of Red Beach 2 for another day, since the conditions at Yellow Beach were shown to be unsuitable for as heavy an inflow as he had intended.

At 1630 Company A was ordered to relieve the advanced elements of Company E and Company G. The latter withdrew to the lagoon shore west of Company A and dug in. About 1830 Company E also retired from an even more advanced position to a line about 300 yards west of the Stone Pier road. In the center of this line, Company A established its perimeter and to the north, next to the lagoon shore, was Detachment Z, 105th Infantry (Map No. 7, p. 100).

For the second night, the naval forces retired from island waters to open sea. Among the men in the slit trenches and the various perimeters, matters were expected to go much as on the preceding night. They braced themselves for the sniping, the ruses, and the endless vigilance so necessary for survival.

In the 3d BLT area near "Rita Lake," at the 105th Field Artillery position on Ukiangong Point, at the western beaches and dumps, and in the Yellow Beach areas occupied by Companies C, D, F, and H, the night brought peace and quiet. Elsewhere, expectations of trouble were fulfilled.

---

[1] So convinced were some of the observers at Makin that Japanese had been using the hulks that they saw enemy fire directed from them at the approaching Alligators and observed the men of the patrol falling under the fire.

Company B spread out to cover the West Tank Barrier. They took precautions which reflected the experience gained on the preceding night. Instead of depending upon rifles, they were instructed to refrain from rifle fire and to throw hand grenades. In front of one platoon, 30 yards of wire clipped from a Japanese trip-line was strung about 2 feet above the ground. Cans were placed to dangle from it, and to sound the alarm if the wire were touched. When three Japanese hit the wire, the barrage of grenades which landed among them killed one and drove the other two in flight to their death on the beach. Four other Japanese dead were found around the Company B perimeter in the morning.

In the line across the island at the east, Company E at one wing and Company G at the other had relatively quiet nights with a short, brisk period of rifle fire against encroaching snipers in the early morning. The men of Company M, 105th Infantry, and Company A, 165th Infantry, in the center and left positions, suffered from grenade and mortar attacks throughout the night. The perimeters had been chosen with care to maintain visual contact and to retain fields of fire before them. Medicine was improvised by the aid station to prevent coughs from breaking the silence and imperiling those in the vicinity. Men who slept were roused at the first signs of snoring. Insect repellents made slapping unnecessary, but, on the other hand, were so strong that they led some of the enemy directly to a target through pitch darkness.

Intelligence gained from captured documents and from the interrogation of prisoners and of natives began to yield a picture of the pre-invasion conditions at Makin which, at the end of the operation, was to be modified only in detail. The enemy consisted of naval ground, air, and labor troops. The naval ground soldiers belonged to the *6th Special Naval Landing Force* of the Yokosuka Naval Base. There were 284 of them on D Day under command of Lt. (jg) Ishikawa. They had come to Makin on 21 September 1942 to replace the garrison so thoroughly destroyed by the night raid of Carlson's Marine Raiders on 16–17 August. Rather separate from them were the air force, including under their control some of the labor troops. Two air units used Makin, the *802d,* which operated "Emilys," and the *952d,* which flew "Nakajima 98" float reconnaissance planes. Personnel totaled 24 in the former and 84 in the latter, on D Day, for the crews had flown out with the 4 planes present as the Northern Landing Force approached. The largest component of labor troops, divided among Koreans and Japanese, had arrived on 15 May 1943 when 300 landed at Makin and were put to work on barracks, roads, fortifications, and the seaplane ramp. Part of the labor troops were the *111th Pioneers,* under a Lieutenant Kurokawa and four lesser officers, while the bulk were in a detachment of the Japanese *Fourth Fleet Construction Department.*

The natives on Butaritari had been expelled from the fortified area between the two tank barriers. Three captured American aviators, who had left before the attack, warned the natives in October to leave Butaritari if they wished to escape a forthcoming battle, but the Japanese forbade the natives to depart for any of the other islands in the atoll group.

The Korean laborers were confined to barracks at night, but their observations during the day had included much of military significance. According to them, occasional freighters and transports, but no enemy warships, appeared at Butaritari. Air Force personnel was inspected semimonthly by an officer who flew in from Jaluit, while supervision of the garrison troops was exercised from Tarawa.

A reconnaissance plane brought warning to Makin's garrison one day before the attack. Troops on the island occupied shelters on both of the nights preceding the actual assault. When that began, the Japanese soldiers took cover in the best places and the Koreans took what was left. The latter remained under cover, although a few accepted an invitation to use arms in defense of the island. Air Force personnel may have left the defense wholly to garrison troops, as some of the prisoners believed, and certainly had abandoned hope of successful resistance by the second day, when several of their officers were discovered in a circle of suicides.

Communications on the island were destroyed by the preparatory bombardment; concerted opposition by the Japanese was reduced to joint action by small groups and lacked a coordinated pattern.

American plans for D + 2 were being worked out as the second day's operations ended. At 1705 General Ralph C. Smith, General Holland M. Smith approving, ordered the 3d BLT to leave the reserve area at daylight and move to the relief of the 2d BLT near the East Tank Barrier. At 0800 it was to attack vigorously, aided by the light and medium tanks, the field artillery, and such naval gunfire and air support as was required. CP's were to move forward

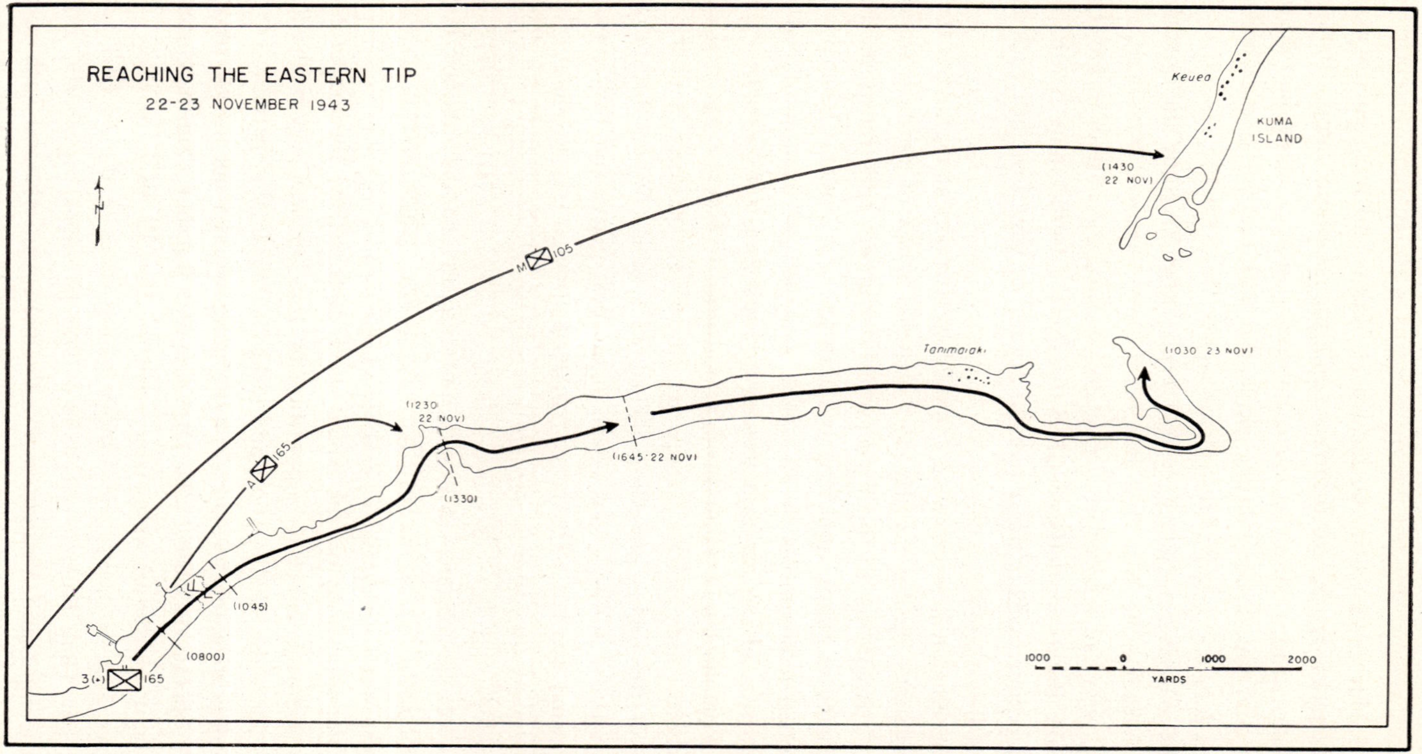

REACHING THE EASTERN TIP

22-23 NOVEMBER 1943

N

Keuea

KUMA
ISLAND

(1430)
22 NOVI

(1010)

(1105)
23 NOVI

Tannmlan

(1645-22 NOVI)

(1230)
22 NOVI

(1330)

A 165

(1045)

(0800)

165

3 (+)

YARDS

1000   0   1000   2000

MAP NO. 8

110

beyond the West Tank Barrier. In the early morning an expedition, guided by Major Herzog, would set out for Kuma Island to intercept any of the enemy who sought refuge there. Another party was to be detached for a less distant encircling movement, going through the lagoon to a point opposite the Bight, and establishing there a strong barrier line across the narrowest point in the island to stop any Japanese fleeing from the pressure of the 3d BLT. Preparations for these movements were made during the night and were greatly aided by a captured map showing trench systems and machine-gun positions. To deny rest to the enemy, harassing artillery fire was dropped in the eastern area from time to time.

The long vigil of another tropical night after two days of battle left the men on Butaritari tense and excitable. At 0400 a sentry on the lagoon convinced himself that some small landing craft out in the lagoon were enemy reinforcements, perhaps from a relieving Japanese task force, which one of the prisoners had reported to be on the way. He roused Colonel Durand and Colonel McDonough in their fox holes near the shore. "There are 200 Japs out there," he reported. Talking very loudly to escape being shot by their own men, the two officers walked to the beach and identified the boats as American.

The Advance Beyond the Bight

At 0600 on the morning of the third day at Makin, the 3d BLT moved along the island highway toward Yellow Beach. Company K elements led the column, a platoon of light tanks followed, and then, in order, Company I, the battalion's antitank platoon, headquarters, and headquarters company (less two platoons), medical units, and Company L in the rear. As the leading units strung out along the highway, an antisubmarine plane from the *Liscombe Bay* began the third day's air support, and at 0619 four planes from the *Corregidor* and seven from the *Coral Sea* started droning over the island on patrol. The ships returned from the open sea. Unloading was resumed on the beaches. The sun rose higher on another clear, hot, humid day.

While the column passed along Yellow Beach, 13 medium tanks and some engineer units fell in. Beyond King's Wharf, Company K swung to the right as far as the ocean, while Company I filled the area at the left to the lagoon, and together they moved ahead in skirmish line. The other elements were in support.

At 0700 artillery on Ukiangong Point started shelling the East Tank Barrier while Companies A, 165th Infantry, and M, 105th Infantry, withdrew. The line moved swiftly ahead across the area taken on the previous afternoon but abandoned during the night. At 0820 the artillery barrage was lifted. The tanks and infantry moved against the enemy. By 0915, the first 250 yards had been crossed with only light opposition. The advance knowledge of machine-gun positions gained from the captured enemy map was helpful to the tanks as they advanced. Resistance became more stubborn as they reached the road running south from Stone Pier (Map No. 9, inside back cover).

The first zone of advance contained a stone church and other buildings, most of them constructed in the period of British occupation before the war. South of them, extending almost all the way to the ocean, were *bobai* pits and marshy gardens associated with the native village of Butaritari. The tanks were obliged to proceed in single file along the highway with the infantry on either wing until the advance reached the Stone Pier road. Then, from the air, they were observed to be spaced abreast along the whole line of advance, and moving forward smoothly.

The tanks shelled the buildings ahead of them, while the infantry grenaded surface installations and small shelters. The combined tactics for the reduction of large shelters, developed in the two preceding days, were employed on four such installations in the zone of Company I, at the left. At 0934 a plane strafed a pillbox on the seaward edge of the tank barrier, while the leading tank was poking its way on to the base of Stone Pier, about 200 yards farther west and across the island.

At the ocean end of the Stone Pier road, and along the shore beyond it, Company K came upon a series of rifle pits and machine-gun nests, with two positions for 70-mm howitzers, of which only one

THIRD BATTALION, *165th Infantry, marching early on 22 November 1943 from the reserve area to continue the eastward attack. On this day they took the East Tank Barrier, advanced beyond the Bight, and when dug in for the night, resisted a series of suicidal attacks.*

EAST TANK BARRIER *system, and its approaches (A). In foreground is Stone Pier with one of the two enemy radar screens at its tip (B). At far left appears part of Government Wharf (C), and opposite it, the clearing for one of the principal Japanese radio installations (D).*

was occupied; these emplacements covered the ocean shore all the way to the East Tank Barrier clearing and its defenses.

At 0945, as the barrier defenses came within range of some of the tanks, the field artillery resumed its barrage also, first on the clearing and then to the east of it. After 25 minutes the shelling from Ukiangong Point stopped. The 105th Field Artillery Battalion then began moving to a new position in the former "citadel" area while the tanks and troops entered the zone which had just been shelled.

With the 3d BLT's attack proceeding relentlessly eastward, Colonel Hart took steps to dam the stream of retiring Japanese by sending a special detachment ahead to stop them. For this mission, two reinforced platoons of Company A, which had spent the night in an advanced perimeter and had then been relieved to rejoin the 1st BLT, were sent with the additional reinforcement of one section of light machine guns and one platoon of heavy machine guns from Company D. The tired troops cleaned their weapons, filled their canteens, and embarked at 1100 in six Alligators under command of Capt. Lawrence J. O'Brien. A 3-mile run over the lagoon would bring them to a landing beach north of the Bight (Map No. 8, p. 110). At that point the island narrowed to a neck 150 yards wide, with a clearing in which machine guns were to be strongly placed.

Shortly after noon they moved from an unopposed beach landing to set up the barrier, and at 1314 reported that, while sustaining no casualties themselves, they had killed or captured 45 of the enemy. They sent to Division Headquarters a friendly English-speaking native who warned of the passage of 40 of the enemy toward the east on the previous afternoon, some of them bearing arms.

Beyond this water-borne, flanking operation, a longer reach was made by Maj. Edward Bradt and a special detail of men from Company M, 105th Infantry. Guided by Major Herzog, they went in ten LVT's to Kuma Island to prevent the retirement there of Japanese fleeing from Butaritari. Although one barge reconnoitered in the middle of the morning, the main movement was delayed until noon, and one of the Alligators became disabled en route. At 1400 the others landed without opposition at the northeastern end of Kuma and worked southwest along it. The ten enemy soldiers who were reported to Major Herzog on the previous day as having hidden on Kuma had already gone farther east. All others would henceforth be sealed on Butaritari as the 3d BLT pressed eastward.

The East Tank Barrier defense system lay, like that at the west, in a clearing among the coconut trees which extended completely across the island. The highway ran through the north end by means of an offset bridge, crossing a wide and deep antitank ditch, and penetrating a break in a large log barrier a few yards farther east. The ditch covered three-fifths of the island's width, in the shape of an open "V" with the point toward the west (see illustration, p. 114). The other southern two-fifths was blocked by a heavy log barricade. West of these structures a curving trench linked a series of three pillboxes, interspersed by six machine-gun emplacements, four antitank emplacements, and over 40 rifle pits. The trench curved away from the advancing troops at the center in a shallow arc. Less than 50 yards in front of the center portion of the firing positions, a set of rifle pits, laid out in approximation of a "U" shape, were the first portion of the defense system to be met.

The combined attack from air, artillery, tank guns, and infantry had reduced the barrier before it was reached. Tanks fired upon the nearest revetments at 0948 and drove forward against the pairs of antitank positions at either end of the system. They passed two very light enemy tankettes (see illustration below), neither of which had

JAPANESE TANKETTE, *one of two found at Makin. Both had been abandoned in revetments and had never been brought into action.*

been moved from its protective bunker, and only one of which was seriously damaged. No fire was received from the antitank positions either, although two 37-mm antitank guns were discovered wrapped in tarpaulins, and fully equipped with ammunition; they had been abandoned in good condition behind the barrier without even being pointed toward the attacking force. On the ocean side, an undamaged 70-mm howitzer was found in position, also unused by the enemy. A few infantrymen cautiously infiltrated through the East Tank Barrier defenses and crossed the clearing unopposed. The rest then took the entire installation at a bound. More heavily fortified than the West Tank Barrier, this defensive system offered far less opposition.

Tanks had passed the barrier and by 1042 were operating in the barracks area between highway and lagoon, 200–300 yards east of the defense system. Two hours later, when the Company A barrier was being thrown across the island neck, the tanks were in a clearing about 800 yards short of that line. The two forces were in communication. The Japanese between the two were about to be caught.

Speedy advance by the 3d BLT brought it to the Company A line at 1330. No opposition, no sniper fire, no captives from either houses or fox holes marked its movement. The enemy remnants had either evaded discovery as the force moved ahead or had slipped east of the island's neck before noon. In the woods beyond the line, natives from a hamlet near the Bight had been hiding. While the 3d BLT rested, about 300 emerged. A cordon of troops surrounded them, and eventually conducted them to the rear. Its 45 minutes of rest over, the battalion resumed its progress toward the tip of the island, still more than 3 miles away, while Company A went to the rear. The easy advance of the 3d BLT had been cautiously executed.

At this stage General Ralph C. Smith, in pursuance of the original plans, assumed full command of the island forces at 1510. He himself went on reconnaissance, as far as the line of advance, and addressed some 200 natives in the village near the Bight through their own magistrate, assuring them of friendship. When he returned to his CP, orders were received from Admiral Turner for the early reëmbarkation of the 1st and 2d BLT's, all the medium tanks, all except five of the light tanks, and all air and naval gunfire liaison officers. General Ralph C. Smith was asked to report as soon as possible his readiness to relinquish command to the commanding officer of the garrison force, Colonel Tenney.

The 3d BLT continued some 2,100 yards beyond the Bight and stopped at 1645 (Map No. 8, p. 110). During the day, it had covered almost three miles of the narrow, bending island strip. The Japanese opposing force consisted of skulking, hidden remnants at best, if not simply of hunted individuals. Estimates of their number, based on what natives said they had seen, were diverse and unreliable, and indicated that many of the survivors were labor troops rather than members of the naval land force. After so little opposition Colonel Hart's battalion settled in for the night with less care than they might have shown had they known what lay before them.

"Saki Night"

Daylight operations on Butaritari closed on the 22d November, the third day of operations, with the various elements of the 27th Division Task Force more widely scattered than on any preceding night. While the ships withdrew according to the standard pattern, and air activity subsided, plans were being made and orders issued for the next day's program. Reëmbarkation was to begin. A captured Japanese marine was to be sent, if possible, to use a public address system to persuade others to give up and to surrender. A reconnaissance was to be made of the remaining islets of the atoll. The day's casualties, 6 dead and 17 wounded or injured, were approximately one-half those of the previous day, while the enemy had lost 99 prisoners and an estimated 100 dead. The operation seemed about complete, with only mopping up to be done. Admiral Turner announced the capture of Makin "though with minor resistance remaining" and congratulated General Ralph C. Smith and his force on their expeditious success.

About 5,000 yards of Butaritari Island remained to be combed for isolated, stranded enemy. Their escape across the reef to Kuma Island at low tide was barred by the expedition under Major Bradt. Late in the afternoon, his force had set up one platoon in a defensive line south of Keuea village, another at the southwestern projection of the island, and a third on the three small outcroppings of the reef to the southeast. The bands of fire obtainable from these positions at the reef made its crossing impossible.

The 3d BLT settled in its company perimeters at the second narrowing of Butaritari Island beyond the Bight. Across the 500 yards of island, the perimeters developed a strong barrier to enemy passage. At the north, Company I covered the lagoon shore, the main island highway, and about 300 yards of the island's width. In an oval clearing in the center of the island, two small ponds intervened between Company I and Company K, which set up a perimeter covering the southern third of the island's width. West of them, in a long, narrow oval running all the way across the island was Company L. On the eastern and western edges of these three positions, and again on the lagoon side of Company I's and the ocean side of Company K's areas, several machine guns were placed, while the highway was covered by two pairs of 37-mm antitank guns, one pair facing east and the other facing west. Company M was split up to support the heavy weapons positions along the eastern fronts of two perimeters.

The men in these three adjacent perimeters had left their entrenching tools with their packs early on this long day and in addition, were dead tired. Their fox holes were shallow, consisting sometimes merely of pieces of coconut log ranged around as a protective bulwark. Positions selected for the mounting of machine guns were chosen with less care for an open field of fire than would have been the case had not the troops, like the higher command, concluded that the enemy were almost eliminated. At several points the undergrowth was thick enough to furnish considerable cover for infiltrating Japanese. The men were instructed not to use rifles, however, except for the repulse of a direct attack.

The enemy came upon them as soon as darkness had fallen. First they sent ahead a party of natives who sought to pass through the perimeter to their hamlet farther west. Then the Japanese themselves came down the road, imitating the cries of a baby in an effort to pass themselves off as another native group until they had reached the American lines. The ruse was recognized, a challenge was given, and machine-gun fire poured among them just before they had deployed.

A little later attempts were made to draw American fire and reveal the location of the antitank guns, machine guns, BAR's, and covering rifles. Although they mounted some machine guns themselves, the Japanese more often came down the road in groups, deployed, and then attacked singly or in small teams. Some infiltrated and fired at forward positions from the rear. Others crawled forward through the underbrush to fire, to draw fire, or to pull in their wounded. Barefoot Japanese ran upon the fox holes and the gun positions, fired at almost point-blank range, and jumped into a melee with the Americans, who killed them with knives or clubbed weapons at the end of a yelling, shouting struggle. Grenades sailed back and forth from one side to another. One sniper, shot out of a tree, landed in a fox hole beneath him occupied by a company commander.

Between attacks, the enemy crawled back to their own lines to drink saki from glasses whose clinking, amid sounds of drunken gaiety, could be heard by the silent and isolated Americans. Some Japanese carried canteens of liquor, and one was found at daylight, standing beneath a tree, alternately shooting a few rounds and singing loudly and unpleasantly. In fox holes beside the guns, wounded, determined Americans soberly held on as their weapons went out of commission and their ammunition ran low. At one point, they could hear a clock with chimes striking the hour in a primitive grass hut close at hand, and thus they were made more strongly aware of the dragging passage of the night. Just before dawn, the oil and patches in a spare-parts kit ignited and burst into flames which illuminated one post. Rifle and machine-gun fire then rained on the spot from the Japanese. At some points, mortar fire also fell.

Daylight alone brought relief. Three dead and 25 wounded lay in the American lines. Fifty-one enemy dead were counted in front of American guns, but the enemy's casualties were not computable, since the wounded had dragged themselves, or been taken, back into the woods to die. All positions remained in the defenders' hands, and the survivors around the pivotal machine guns and antitank guns on the left flank, who had been engaged throughout the night, rejoined their units when they formed up for the advance. The Japanese action on what came to be known as "Saki Night" may have been "heavy patrolling," or "banzai attacks," but it was the last concerted resistance by an utterly desperate remnant of the original Japanese force.

Some of the enemy tried to move out of the swamps south of Tanimaiaki village that night by crossing the reef to Kuma Island. At midnight about ten of them approached the 105th Infantry detail's defense line there and were either killed or wounded in the attempt to cross. Unless others had gone beyond Kuma before the detail arrived, the last vestiges of the original Japanese forces were destined to be pinched off on 23 November, D + 3.

The Island's Tip Is Reached

On the fourth day of the Makin operation, as preparations for the withdrawal of the Northern Landing Force began, regimental headquarters awoke from a calm night to discover that its wire communications with the 3d BLT were broken. In ignorance of "Saki Night," headquarters prepared a detail to appeal over a loudspeaker to the group of Japanese believed to be hiding near Tanimaiaki village and to invite them to surrender. The village lay at the eastern end of the island highway, on the lagoon shore, and beyond it, like a large "V" lying on its side, the island came to its easternmost tip and bent back, northwestward, around an inlet of the lagoon.

The medium tanks returned from bivouac to join the 3d BLT near the Bight, and their movement had broken the line to regimental headquarters. The tired battalion formed for the drive ahead to the tip, and to mop up what remained of the enemy in nearly four miles of narrowing, zigzagging island. In a light tank, 1st Lt. John T. Farley, artillery S–2, reconnoitered Tanimaiaki village without seeing the enemy or receiving a shot. An advance party, Company I, was sent along the road to the village to comb the region beyond it. As many as possible clambered on the outsides of the tanks, 5 lights and 16 mediums, and rode slowly forward, while the rest of the men trudged along the highway on foot.

Behind them, Company K on the left and Company L on the right formed a skirmish line across the island and moved out at 0715. Behind them were the men of Company B, 1st BLT, who had been sent forward as a reserve support. With the left-wing elements rode a Nisei broadcasting detail in a jeep with 2d Lt. John E. Allen, USMC, and Lt. Col. S. L. A. Marshall, historical officer. They had come up to the CP just as the battalion was about to start, and had found Colonel Hart convinced that a group of active enemy were ahead of them, and might be encountered at the village. When they reached the village at 0945, however, no enemy was there, and only occasional sniper fire had been met. An appeal to surrender was deemed useless; in the absence of communications, the detail took a message back to regimental headquarters reporting the night's fighting, the existing situation, and Colonel Hart's belief that support might be needed later. On its return, after 2 uneventful miles along the highway, the jeep came under sniper fire for about 300 yards, and shortly afterward found friendly troops from Company L.

The skirmish line had been moving cautiously for about 600 yards when the center encountered a nest of snipers firing from the trees. The enemy fire caught the 2d and 3d Platoons, Company L, trying to spread out enough to reëstablish contact between them. Three men were killed and the others were pinned down. Tank support was requested by Capt. Martin E. Nolan, company commander; while it

was coming, the 1st Platoon pushed on alone for a mile and a half next to the ocean shore. Two light tanks under 2d Lt. George P. Evans joined the 2d and 3d Platoons, and after silencing the enemy, tanks and infantry moved together to the left, went along the highway, and came up to the line of the 1st Platoon. A portion of the island was thus very lightly combed. By 1000, their advance brought them to a second aggregation of snipers, that past which the broadcasting detail had just driven.

TANKS RETURN FROM EASTERN BUTARITARI *after pushing with 3d Bn to island's tip on 23 November 1943. Enemy resistance has dropped to scattered, desperate parties. Medical aid crew waits beside the highway with its jeep while No. 19 (S/Sgt. Doyle Major) rolls past.*

Two miles farther the advance party of tanks and riflemen from Company I, after passing beyond Tanimaiaki village at about 0900, stopped while the riders dismounted and turned into the woods to the south. To search the area in detail, Company I formed a skirmish line. Company K overtook the line and filled in its right side, along the ocean. They proceeded for 2,000 yards out to the easternmost tip and then back, northwest, to the very end of Butaritari Island. After crossing a crudely built coral causeway, they came upon an air-raid shelter in which a grenade and 37-mm fire from the tanks killed two of the enemy. About 200 yards farther a second shelter was encountered near the ocean shore. It was rather lightly constructed, and after Capt. John J. Walsh of Company K had crawled forward and tossed in a grenade, 2d Lt. Lloyd Welsh and Sgt. Robert L. McCoy, Jr., removed the top logs and exposed nine stunned Japanese. They were disposed of by thorough rifle fire, which killed one who had been shamming.

A smaller detail investigated a tongue of land which projected into the lagoon northeast of the village. There they found only one enemy officer, asleep.

At 1030 the forward units of the 3d BLT reached the extremity of the island. They had found and killed three of the exhausted enemy in the woods, but in the remaining underground shelters had discovered only caches of food. As they looked across a mile of shoal water to the small islets and the tip of Kuma, they could feel that the task force had attained its objective. "Makin taken," General Ralph C. Smith reported to Admiral Turner. "Recommend command pass to commander garrison force."

A JAPANESE PRISONER, *one of three Japanese and 101 Koreans captured, going to Command Post at Ukiangong village for interrogation.*

The End of the Makin Expedition

Preparations for Departure

THE FOURTH DAY'S OPERATIONS ON MAKIN included mopping-up activities and the initial stage of arrangements for departure. The eastern end of Butaritari was combed; other islands of the atoll were reconnoitered; and at Yellow Beach and Red Beach 2, the service forces labored with extraordinary activity. The withdrawal from Makin was being hastened.

Enemy air activity was expected to increase. Repeated bombings of air bases in the Marshalls and on Nauru prevented the use of the nearer Japanese fields, while radar detection and intercepting formations from naval carriers had protected the operations at Makin from attack by long-range enemy planes. Only against night torpedo bombing attacks had the defense been insufficient, and the enemy had preferred to deliver them off Tarawa.

Japanese submarines had been detected by antisubmarine patrols and by the underwater sound apparatus of surface ships. It was

believed that others were to reach the Gilberts area on 24 November. An early departure of the ships off Makin was required by Admiral Turner. At 1730 on the third day, General Ralph C. Smith was requested to prepare his troops for reëmbarkation at dawn.

Much remained to be done before the island could be left in suitable condition for the garrison force. Care for the wounded and the dead, including the almost intolerably noisome, unburied enemy dead; disposition of enemy prisoners and captured matériel; unloading of that which was still on the transports and which would be needed by the portion of the original expedition which was to remain with the garrison force; separation of equipment to be left temporarily for the use of occupying troops; reloading of what was to return to Oahu on the transports; unloading from the LST's of high-priority antiaircraft ordnance and construction equipment; disposal of unexploded bombs and shells; provision for the personnel to be left behind—all required attention on the fourth day at Makin.

The wounded had been taken from the aid stations to the transports until the clearing station at Ukiangong village was in readiness at noon of the second day. During the afternoon 15 casualties were brought to the station, and before the expedition had departed from Makin, 59 more came in. Three of these died, but 13 were quickly returned to duty. The transports also received 74 casualties directly, almost all of them before the clearing station had opened. From the total of 160 Army and Marine personnel wounded in action, 40 were evacuated by air, being taken across the lagoon to a seaplane, flown to Funafuti, transferred there to an Army Air Forces transport, and conveyed to Oahu, the whole journey requiring about 24 hours.

Two cemeteries were created for American dead. In the "Gate of Heaven" cemetery near Ukiangong village, 39 were buried, and in "Sleepy Lagoon" cemetery near Yellow Beach, 21. Boatswain Kaspar and an unidentified naval crewman from the *Alcyone* were buried on a point on Kotabu Island. The Army graves registration officer and two enlisted men remained with the rear detachment.

Enemy dead numbered over 400, scattered all over the island. On the second day a burial party had been organized among the natives, who had been collected on Flink Point under Maj. Robert K. Ryland and Capt. John P. Collins of the USMC. About 50 natives worked at this task, and had completed about a third of it when the day's work ended. To hasten it to completion, the ditch in the West Tank

Barrier system was used for a common grave. Enemy shelters were also collapsed and sealed by bulldozers. At the time of departure, the eastern part of Butaritari remained to be treated.[1]

Prisoners were gathered on the *Leonard Wood* from the other transports and from the cages ashore. Only 3 of them were Japanese; the remaining 101 were Korean laborers. (See illustration, p. 125.) Captured matériel was classified and disposed of in several ways. Weapons and equipment valuable for military study were boxed for reloading. Since this work had not been completed when the convoy departed, a detail consisting of 1st Lt. Ward T. Gilbert and 12 enlisted men was left in charge of it. The two Japanese tankettes were placed aboard the *Alcyone,* but lesser weapons and even enemy documents were the objects of competition between the souvenir hunters and the intelligence staff. A thorough G–2 study of the defenses on Butaritari was made.

Captured vehicles, sedans, trucks, and motorcycles were converted to the use of the garrison. Engineer supplies, notably cement, iron rails, and lumber, were put under guard for use by the construction crews soon to arrive, while food and clothing were either given out, or stored for later distribution, to the natives.

The fresh water which had been brought with the expedition had supplied the troops during the first 4 days, while an evaporator and purifier were put into operation near Red Beach and accumulated 2,000 gallons in storage there. Before the departure, a 10,000-gallon evaporator was brought ashore and set up on the ocean side of the island across from Yellow Beach, and in addition, three smaller units were either ashore or awaiting their turns to be unloaded from LST's.

Speedy reloading of the transports was facilitated by freedom to dispense with combat loading and to separate troops from combat equipment which they might use. It was, however, impeded by the necessity of withdrawing the ships in the evening and by the fact that for only a few daylight hours was the tide full enough to permit ample use of Yellow Beach. By Admiral Turner's orders, Yellow

---

[1] Hygienic conditions on the island were left in an unsatisfactory condition by the departing force. Among the troops of the garrison a mild form of dengue fever was rampant, and by the first week of January, bacillary dysentery was epidemic. Flies had multiplied amid the fecal and other matter left promiscuously during combat. The epidemic was brought under control quickly by standard methods.

Beach was used for almost all the reloading as well as the continued unloading operations.

Reëmbarkation

At 1400 on 23 November, the 2d BLT under Colonel MacDonough started reëmbarkation at Red Beach 2. They had marched along the main island highway from bivouac near Yellow Beach, crossed the West Tank Barrier, passed the site where Colonel Conroy had been killed, and reversed the route by which the western landing units had moved to meet the 2d BLT on the first day of battle. Entering the landing barges, they pushed out to the *Pierce* against 4-foot swells; they were to spend the next ten days aboard her.

From 1900 to 2120 that evening, and again during the next morning, the 27th Division staff and the improvised staff of Colonel Tenney, garrison force commander, conferred. They arranged the transfer to him of command, which was set at 0800 on 24 November, and the release, for use by his force, of matériel which it would need. The main elements of his command were to arrive at 1100 on 24 November and would not be ashore when the assault troops departed.

COLUMN MARCHING TOWARD YELLOW BEACH *to reëmbark. 2d BLT had gone from Red Beach 2 aboard* Pierce *late on 23 November. Other elements, like 1st BLT here, reëmbarked next morning. The Task Force sailed in early afternoon, leaving 3d Battalion in defense force.*

A considerable quantity of communications equipment already in operation, with the personnel to use it, was left behind until such activities could be assumed by the permanent garrison. All the Alligators and the 1 dukw were left, and with them, a navy boat pool of 9 officers and 194 enlisted men. Many of the trucks, bulldozers, and jeeps remained also.

The desire to hasten departure was strengthened by the disaster with which the fifth day's operations began. At 0510 the aircraft carrier *Liscombe Bay* was struck by a torpedo from an enemy submarine while her planes were being readied for flight at dawn. Explosions and fierce fires caused her to sink in 20 minutes, surrounded by flaming oil. Losses included about 80 percent of her complement, among them Rear Adm. Henry M. Mullinnix, commanding the Air Support Group (TG 52.3), and Capt. I. D. Wiltsie, in command of the ship. While survivors were being picked up and brought to the transports, reloading operations were expedited.

The 1st BLT under Major Mahoney went aboard the *Calvert* during the morning, while other detachments were being carried to other transports. (See illustration, p. 128.) At noon the special detail from Kuma Island arrived just in time to board the *Leonard Wood,* following the headquarters staff. The troops carried as much equipment as possible with them, but in the haste of departure, not all the desired matériel could be brought to the beach, or, if there, be conveyed to the transports. That which was left was marked for reloading and left in care of the rear detachment.

The 3d BLT remained for the assistance and protection of the construction forces, along with Battery C, 105th Field Artillery; one platoon of Company C, 193d Tank Battalion; the Alligator detachment from Headquarters Company, 193d Tank Battalion; the Collecting Platoon and the Clearing Company and surgical team, 102d Medical Battalion; Company C, 102d Engineers; the 152d Engineers; Batteries K and L, 93d Coast Artillery (AA), Batteries A, B, C, and D, 98th Coast Artillery (AA), and the I and R Platoon, 165th Infantry.

At noon the convoy was prepared to start the trip back to Oahu but was held until after 1400 by threat of attack from enemy airplanes which had been spotted about ten miles away. It was the sixth air raid alarm of the operation. The convoy consisted of the same transports which had brought the Northern Landing Force to Makin before dawn on 20 November, and, as protecting elements, warships which needed repairs, like the battleship *Mississippi* and two destroyers from Tarawa. By 2 December, most of the ships had arrived at Oahu, the men having rested, cleaned up, and taken careful stock of their combat experiences, unit by unit.

Mopping Up

On 24 November, when the convoy was getting started, the I and R Platoon completed an overnight investigation of the islands comprising Little Makin without discovering any enemy refugees. The chief of the islanders, who lived there, received a formal visit from the expedition. His people were entirely friendly.

The 3d BLT also sent a reconnoitering detail to the islets of the northwestern corner of Makin atoll early on 24 November, while the main body of the battalion organized the defense of Butaritari from enemy counterattack.

AIRFIELD CONSTRUCTION EQUIPMENT *is being unloaded from LST's at end of King's Wharf. Makin is to become an air base. Its capture is intended not only to deny it to the enemy but also to yield an airstrip from which to launch air strikes upon him at other points.*

When the Northern Landing Force left, work had already begun on an airstrip 4,000 by 400 feet, which was expected to be in operation 3 weeks later, and to be extended by another 2,000 feet if needed. (See illustration, p. 130.) Two fighter squadrons and one fighter-bomber squadron were to use Makin as a base, where provision was planned for 50 fighter planes and 25 fighter-bombers on hardstands of coral pavement. The additional forces for service and defense would aggregate over 5,500 men.

Japanese resistance had not been totally suppressed simply by sweeping Butaritari from west to east and reconnoitering other islands. The 3d BLT, for example, had cleared the island to its eastern tip, as described, during 23 November, after which it retired for its fourth night there to the vicinity of the Bight. It organized a defensive perimeter and settled down. At dusk along the highway from the west came seven Japanese who were dispersed by machine-gun fire. From the east others approached, of whom eight were killed and two were wounded. Still other Japanese who had somehow remained concealed from the invaders appeared that night on the reef between Butaritari and Kuma; five of them were killed as they tried to cross. Among the Kuma Island detail which barred passage across the reef, enemy rifle, machine-gun, and mortar fire fell, killing three and wounding nine.

The natives engaged in burying enemy dead came upon at least two unwounded live Japanese among the dead occupants of deep shelters. From time to time during the next few weeks, small parties and individuals committed suicide or made suicidal attacks upon the garrison. The main portion of the Northern Landing Force had already spent one day back in Oahu when 9 of the enemy fought 13 American soldiers on Butaritari until only 3 Japanese were left to flee in safety.

Tanks as well as infantry patrolled the possible places of enemy refuge. Two weeks after the assault forces retired, a handful of the enemy still roved the island at night, keeping away from American patrols, and surviving despite the scarcity of water and food. "Today looks like another clear day," wrote the executive officer of the Japanese force in his diary on 11 December. "I feel like singing a song. There is a breeze coming from the northwest. I hope the tanks won't come today, so that I can rest my body in peace." One more day was to pass before his troubles were over.

Conclusion

THE COST OF CAPTURING MAKIN in casualties among Army personnel was not great; 58 killed in action, 8 died of wounds, 150 wounded in action, and 35 injured, but not in combat.[1] At Tarawa, losses were much more severe among the more numerous assault forces: 913 killed and missing, and 2,037 wounded, among the Marines; 26 killed and 48 wounded, among the Navy. At Makin, moreover, the Navy losses greatly exceeded those of the Army. During the preparatory bombardment on D Day, a turret fire on the *Mississippi* killed 40 men and injured 9. In the boat crews and the beach parties, seven were wounded or injured, while three died of wounds. Combat and operational losses on 8 carriers, not including the ill-fated *Liscombe Bay,* totaled 7 killed and 18 injured. The submarine *Plunger,* on rescue patrol, while picking up a flier from the *Lexington,* was strafed by Japanese planes, and six of its crew were wounded. Finally, when the *Liscombe Bay* went down, 702 men were lost and her 257 survivors were taken aboard the transports in various stages of injury, principally from burns. Besides the loss of the carrier itself and 19 planes based on it, 9 other planes were lost in combat and 35 in operational mishaps. Consolidated naval casualties were, then, 752 killed or died of wounds, 291 wounded or injured, 63 planes lost, and one escort carrier sunk.

For this expenditure at Makin, and by the battle of Tarawa and the unopposed seizure of Apamama, the American forces obtained strategic advantages which had been anticipated. Shorter lines to the Southwest Pacific could now be maintained and Japanese interference with them could be more readily neutralized. A base was gained for operations against the Marshall Islands.

---

[1] Army casualties were distributed as follows: infantry, 178; tank corps, 25; engineers, 21; medical corps, 9; field artillery, 6; coast artillery (AA), 3; signal corps, 3; air corps, 1; unidentified, 5.

In the fighting which lay ahead, the Army derived another advantage from its capture of Makin. From that experience in taking a Pacific atoll it learned valuable lessons. Participants in the Makin campaign, from higher levels of command to the smallest combat units, sifted their observations and submitted reports and recommendations.

In reviewing the operation, the participants recognized that the tactical plan had, on the whole, been vindicated by the results. Certain errors on which it had been based seemed when analyzed to offset each other. The fact that the beaches were all incapable of efficient use was balanced by the enemy's weakness, even greater than had been anticipated. He was not able to oppose the landings effectively nor to strike the beaches from the air during the period preceding their defense by antiaircraft artillery. The expectation that the enemy could be enveloped by first attacking from the west and then sending one BLT to strike his rear from Yellow Beach was not realized, for he did not move out to oppose the invasion from the west with the main body of his forces. Nevertheless, whatever plan of defense may have existed was disorganized by the prearranged fire, the air strikes, and the double attack; some of the enemy artillery was not even used on D Day, and the firing upon the waves approaching Yellow Beach was so badly delivered as to inflict surprisingly few casualties.

Improved preliminary reconnaissance, particularly the close examination of beach conditions and more thorough air photographic coverage, was indicated as necessary by the experience at Makin. So, also, was a heavier and more concentrated prearranged fire, as much as ten times heavier if the Japanese underground shelters were to be destroyed.

The main problem in capturing Makin was, as had been anticipated, that of coordinating the attacking force employed, a problem rendered peculiarly difficult by the cramped space of Butaritari. All support tended to become close support. Flat terrain and limited area made control of fire abnormally difficult. Artillery spotting had to be done from the air. The marked improvement during the first day's action in tank-infantry cooperation was held to indicate that such teamwork could exist from the outset if training were sufficient. In fact, recommendations from all sides called for longer training exercises, under circumstances similar to a forthcoming operation, by the actual personnel using the very material which was to be employed against the enemy. Infantry, tanks, aircraft carriers, air-ground liaison, shore fire control, transports, ship and shore parties—all were to benefit from such joint training. Practice in using the actual communications plan would, moreover, familiarize personnel with the frequencies, the nets, and the possibilities of error, as well as the available emergency rearrangements of facilities. Certain improvements to be gained by infantry training were indicated, including dispersion during landings, regard for cover during ground advance, maintenance of contact and the protection of flanks, avoidance of indiscriminate firing, and development of the spirit of combat.

Air evacuation of the wounded from a combat zone was reported to be justifiable only when the sick bays of the transports and hospital ships were overcrowded.

The sequence among the landing waves by which first Alligators and then tanks crossed the beaches ahead of the infantry was recommended for future operations. For landing under fire, armor was proposed in the newly designed Alligators, and for efficiency, a ramp at one end. To facilitate communication by ground troops with the crews of tanks, when hatches were all closed, it was suggested that a telephone be installed on the rear of each tank.

Better waterproofing of equipment, from radios to vehicles, was shown to be necessary. For the radios, a waterproof container which was secure without inducing internal condensation was requisite. BAR's, flame throwers, and hand grenades were warmly endorsed, but the carbine was suspected of sounding too much like the Japanese rifle to make its use in Pacific fighting desirable.

At Makin, then, the reports by participants declared, the preparatory naval gunfire and aerial bombing, the selection of beaches, the initial coordination among tanks and ground troops, the performance of communications elements, and the "indiscriminate" fire over the flat terrain were all faulty. The men were said to have carried much burdensome, useless equipment ashore. Yet capacity for adjustment to all situations, and ability to improvise in the presence of unforeseen difficulties, were employed with conspicuous success. Combat experience converted the 27th Division Task Force into battlewise troops. Like the victors at Tarawa, they emerged from the capture of the Gilberts better prepared for later advances along the new "road to Tokyo."

Seventh Air Force

V Amphibious Corps

27th Division

ANNEX NO. I

Abbreviations

AKA	Cargo Vessel, Attack
APA	Transport, Attack
BAR	Browning Automatic Rifle
BLT	Battalion Landing Team
Bn (C)	Combat Battalion
CV	Aircraft Carrier
CVE	Aircraft Carrier, Escort
CVL	Aircraft Carrier, Large
I and R Platoon	Intelligence and Reconnaissance
LCM	Landing Craft, Mechanized
LCT	Landing Craft, Tank
LCV	Landing Craft, Vehicle
LCVP	Landing Craft, Vehicle, Personnel
LSD	Landing Ship, Dock
LST	Landing Ship, Tank
LVT	Landing Vehicle, Tracked
RCT	Regimental Combat Team
RJ	Road Junction
TF	Task Force
TG	Task Group
XAK	Cargo Vessel (Auxiliary)
XAP	Transport (Auxiliary)

☆ U. S. GOVERNMENT PRINTING OFFICE : 1946—692414